For those who have taught me the most about difficult conversations:

Melanie Morrison
  —for whom struggle and grace
      powerfully reinforce each other;

The Class of 1999, Lutheran Theological Seminary at Philadelphia
  —whose risk-taking and trust-making in the classroom
      go with them in their ministries; and

Gerard Cooney
  —whose loving acceptance and Kiwi honesty
      can turn fireside chats into deepening dialogue.

Difficult conversations

taking risks, acting with integrity

KATIE DAY

THE ALBAN INSTITUTE

Library of Congress Card Number 00-111199

ISBN 1-56699-239-7

As with most books, this work represents a collaborative effort. However, in writing about conversations, I have been acutely aware throughout the process how very indebted I am to the many conversation partners who have contributed directly and indirectly to the ideas that found their way into print.

I am especially grateful to the Lutheran Theological Seminary at Philadelphia, where I have taught since 1985. The faculty and administration had the sensitivity to recognize a subtle trend in congregations and religious institutions—that is, that faithful members were talking less and less to each other about difficult issues. In renewing the curriculum in the 1990s, they had the vision and commitment to shape a required course in which seminarians would learn how to engage and cultivate real conversation around the most troubling issues that deserved not neglect, but the best resources of the community of faith. I was privileged to teach the course for the first time to the extraordinary class of 1999.

Not only did those students sink their teeth into the course, but they shaped it for future classes. In addition, they continued well after that fall semester to engage courageously in difficult conversation and the acts of integrity to which such conversations often lead. A group of these students, now pastors, have continued to provide wise insight and constructive feedback on the words and ideas presented here. I especially want to thank Steve Keiser, Maggie Spring, Jennifer Hitt, Scott Paradise, Peggy Wuertele, and Tom Maehl. Their congregations are gifted by the creativity, honesty, and chutzpah of these new, yet seasoned pastors.

We were not the only religious community to take note of the declining engagement with tough issues on the part of people of faith. At about the same time Melanie and Eleanor Morrison—an unusual mother-daughter team, the founders and directors of Leaven, a center for reflection in Michigan—were bringing women of both African and European descent together to talk about race. The program, as painful as it was transformative, was called "Difficult Conversations." Their work has long been an inspiration to me, and their appropriate title soon became the tag for the course at our school.

Many others contributed suggestions and critiques along the way. Their insights were almost always illuminating to me. I am grateful to John Steinbruck, who has been teaching the course recently not only because I have been writing but also because he has embodied difficult conversations throughout his ministry. I also benefited from the careful reading and honest feedback of Phil Day, who brought his own courage and integrity to the task.

Beth Gaede made the manuscript stronger through her perceptive editing and made me a better writer through her patient persistence.

Finally, and foremost, I am thankful for my best conversation partner in life, Gerard Cooney. Without the gift of many, many late-night conversations by the fire, I know that I would explore far fewer ideas and take far fewer risks in conversation. Our children, Julian and Molly, have a knack for asking the impertinent questions as well as the pertinent ones. Children are God's gift to grown-ups who might find their conversation muscles getting slack, and I am thankful that they constantly remind me of the need to learn new language.

CHAPTER 1

Difficult Conversations

The seminary amphitheater was packed for one of the fall convocation lectures. Future pastors and church leaders sat shoulder to shoulder at long tables on elevated tiers in a horseshoe facing the podium. Latecomers were forced to sit in the aisles or stand in the back. The presenter brilliantly addressed the church's role in public health, stressing the need for the community of faith to advance health services to older people and to provide caring support to those living with HIV/AIDS. At the conclusion, hands went up and students asked polite questions of clarification, theological nuance, or effective strategies. Responding to one question, the lecturer referred to "protecting a woman's right to choose." Immediately a young woman's hand shot up. Without waiting to be called on, she blurted out, "But of course in the church we oppose abortion and want to protect the rights of the unborn!" A brief, awkward silence ensued, broken only by the barely perceptible collective gasp of the audience. The speaker then called on another student, who asked about provisions in the denomination's health coverage for clergy.

The hapless student looked confused, if not shocked, then closed her dropped jaw. She was obviously a first-year student and not yet socialized into seminary culture. She would soon learn that *we don't talk about controversial issues here.* No matter that a diversity of thinking may have prevailed in the community on the subject of abortion. No matter that she had given voice to the thoughts of many—even among the majority who decidedly favored abortion rights, as well as those who were unresolved on the issue. No matter that those within the mainline Protestant community pride themselves on tolerance of diversity and affirm the ongoing revelation of God's will through the people in every time and place.

My mind drifted back to my own seminary days when lunches in the cafeteria often went uneaten as we debated women's ordination. Passions could run high in classroom discussions over strictly theological issues such as the authority of the Bible, lifestyle matters like consumerism, moral conflicts over tax resistance, public-policy questions of nuclear energy or Central America. We waded into sticky multidimensional issues like homosexuality, which were at once theological, moral, personal and public. Often women were less comfortable entering into such debates in larger classes—a reality that fortunately is changing—but would explore the same issues in smaller groups, often late into the night in dorm rooms or apartments or over coffee. Of course, memories get revised, and the past can be romanticized. The passionate conversations of my seminary years were not shining examples of well-reasoned argument articulated in polished language. Often the arguments were spurious, the language awkward; the ideas we explored were sometimes wacky. But conversational muscles were being exercised.

In recent years many have bemoaned the fact that communities of faith are noticeably absent from the public forum. Why is it, Yale law professor and writer Stephen Carter and others have asked, that religious voices have historically been heard in public debates—on slavery, civil rights and the Vietnam War—advocating for progressive social change? Yet in more recent years a faith perspective has rarely been heard in the social struggles over current issues such as welfare reform, military interventions (like the Gulf War) or gun control. Despite denominational policy statements on these issues, advocacy is seldom seen or heard beyond the staff of the Washington offices of the mainline Protestant groups. Carter theorizes that the stridency of the religious right, particularly in relation to abortion, has effectively silenced others from articulating alternative positions or even entering into public dialogue from a faith perspective. Even individuals of deep faith may speak out as good citizens but bury their religious language out of fear that they too could be identified with "extremists" who "wear their religion on their sleeve." Many in the so-called mainline Protestant community assume that the faith-based advocates who enter the public debate tend to be sure of their positions and well organized. Even though for most churchgoers faith is an important resource in shaping our social convictions, we are not unequivocal in our understanding of an issue and united in our stand. Issues are messy. We appreciate that a diversity of opinion exists even within the community of faith. We are less certain that our faith-informed perspective should universally prevail, nor do we have a well-heeled organization backing us up. The effect of the powerful voice of the religious right, Carter says, has been to inhibit rather than to invite dialogue, especially among other people of faith.

Perhaps he is right, or perhaps we project too much power onto the religious right to explain our own shortcomings.

Sociologist Robert Putnam offers another explanation. In his recent book *Bowling Alone*,[1] he presents a compelling collection of data pointing to a demonstrable decline in American culture of what he calls *social capital*—that is, all the ways people develop connections with each other. By all counts, he finds, Americans are venturing less and less beyond their families to join clubs, write letters, participate in community meetings, go to picnics, attend churches, and, yes, join bowling leagues. His wide and eclectic research findings support his general pessimistic thesis:

> For the first two-thirds of the twentieth century a powerful tide bore Americans into ever deeper engagement in the life of their communities, but a few decades ago—silently, without warning—that tide reversed and we were overtaken by a treacherous rip current. Without at first noticing, we have been pulled apart from one another and from our communities over the last third of the century.[2]

It is not just people of faith who refrain from entering into public debate—a general tendency toward civic disengagement cuts across all sectors of society. Not only are voting rates declining precipitously (two-thirds of voters turned out for the 1960 presidential election; fewer than half did in 1996), but all forms of participation in democratic deliberation have declined. Fewer and fewer Americans are writing letters to the local newspaper or to their congressional representatives. Fewer are attending community meetings, volunteering for political organizations, or even signing petitions—all critical building blocks for a robust democracy. The alarming diagnosis: "In effect more than a third of America's civic infrastructure simply evaporated between the mid-1970's and the mid-1990's."[3]

In this wider social context we see also the disengagement of the church and its individual members from public deliberation. Not many Americans are enthusiastically fueling the engine of democracy through activities that would further our corporate conversation, so why should the church be any different? Aren't we simply one thread in a larger social fabric?

Yes—and no. That the church is embedded in the wider culture cannot be ignored. Yet we often live in the illusion that we are not unduly influenced by our cultural contexts—local, regional, national, racial/ethnic, and class, to name a few. However,

when we observe the church in Korea or El Salvador or South Africa, we can clearly see how much culture shapes the way *those* people understand and express their faith. But we are less insightful when it comes to ourselves. Social scientists build entire careers documenting the ways that culture shapes our patterns of believing and belonging. Like it or not, social location does influence the construction and expression of faith. Where we sit affects where we stand.

On the other hand, the myth that our communities of faith in North America somehow transcend culture is not entirely self-deception. We affirm in our gathering each week that in fact the church is not merely one thread in the social fabric but a people "called out" (*ecclesia*) to worship and follow the Creator God who moves in, yet beyond, all cultures. We understand that our collective identity is being

5

shaped by a divine potter and cannot be reduced to a social construction. We hope and believe that those who gather as people of God are not entirely captive to our culture and have a spiritual capacity to be a unique presence in society. We have the audacity to believe that the Spirit of God can give us a critical perspective on ourselves and our cultures, and further enable us to participate in the transformation of both.

Even Robert Putnam sees religious communities as having a unique presence within a society that is busy unloading its social capital.[4] Despite his data indicating that religion is also on the track of becoming more privatistic and less social (with a few notable exceptions), Putnam appreciates the resources that faith communities bring to the daunting project of reversing the trend. In his historical analysis of periods of civic revival in American history, he notes the major role that religion has played. He then offers a challenge to communities of faith to mine our resources (dare we say "spiritual capital?") to help bring about social transformation—that is, another period of civic engagement.

Dialogue Begins at Home

The adult Sunday school class of Hillside United Church, a large suburban congregation, obviously enjoyed being together. The 20 or so participants greeted each other warmly and asked about one another's families. Their morning discussion was marked by elbow jabbing, teasing, and laughing at jokes known only to them. The one African American member was kidded about not needing sunscreen, and she responded with a familiar but weary chuckle.

They moved through the scheduled lesson with dispatch and spent the rest of their time telling the guest in the group about their many activities and their special bond. These were not lonely bowlers—social capital was running high. Their activities were diverse and impressive. Their résumé included not only the traditional fare of Bible study and potlucks, but also the production of full-length original musicals. After enthusiastically describing the group's history and dynamics, they drew a collective breath and summarized themselves as what one called "just a big, wonderful family." Another member added, "We can talk about anything here!"

Clearly this group was active, although not activist. The primary value was social, so it was not surprising that they had not been involved in public issues. But could they talk about them? What we define as social issues—from poverty to nuclear energy to sexuality—are finally personal issues, which become collectivized as individuals struggle with their own needs and everyone else's as well. Because these members could look out their church windows and see nuclear cooling towers in the landscape, I asked if they ever talked about nuclear energy. Because they were located near a large city, I wondered if they ever discussed suburban sprawl, the exodus of urban jobs to the outer rings, or the current public debate about regionalism (the need for city and suburbs to share resources). These topics had never come up. Perhaps they were too political for the nature of this group. I moved closer to home. Had they ever talked about racism? Homosexuality? Domestic violence? Unemployment? The status of women? Public versus private schooling? Abortion? This group, whose members considered themselves family, had never had conversation about any of these subjects, although it was a safe bet that all these issues were

7

present within the congregation. These were not abstract issues relegated to the political sector or explored only in the media. While not every family in the church had dealt with every issue named, it was a safe prediction that these were not struggles seen only on TV's "Oprah Winfrey Show." These problems touched the lives of members to the same degree that they were present throughout society. After church, the African American member came up and quietly thanked me for bringing the word "racism" into the group.

Lest we rush too quickly rush to judgment about this group of believers who were at once committed to their faith and to one another, we have to recognize how familiar the scenario is. We know this group. We're in it.

Congregations in all traditions gather regularly to engage in the profound and intimate activity of seeking to know and worship God. Commitment can run high in faith communities. Members support each other through significant life transitions—birth, marriage, the loss of a loved one, and death itself. Yet congregations do not engage in difficult conversations around the issues that trouble us both as individuals and as a society. These messy issues, which consume much of our energy and resources and need the best of collective wisdom to move toward resolution, are strangely missing from our conversation. If difficult conversations cannot happen in the congregation—then where? Should there not be a basis of trust in our faith community on which we can rely to try out new ideas and work through confusion? Why we avoid difficult conversations in our congregations is not immediately apparent; but it is clear that when we attempt it in our larger gatherings we often do it badly. Messy issues can result in denominational messes; personal pain becomes aggregated into institutional bruises. If athletes do not consistently train at home, they will get clobbered in national competition and won't stand a chance in the Olympics. If we do not exercise our conversational ability in our small communities of faith, we will not be ready for the big leagues.

Perhaps the best explanation of the church's reticence in the public forum is not that the religious right has taken center stage and silenced the rest of us, but that we have lost the capacity to talk to each other in significant ways. If we can't engage in difficult conversations in our local communities of faith, why would anyone expect the religious community to assume an effective and larger role as actor in democratic deliberations over public issues? Public and congregational dialogue is related. In fact, Nancy Ammerman, a sociologist at Hartford Seminary, found in her extensive study of churches in changing communities that congregations whose members can accommodate conflict in healthy ways among themselves are more likely to engage community issues productively.[5]

It is in congregations, among sisters and brothers in the faith, that we can begin to exercise the conversational muscles needed for civic engagement. It is here that we can learn a language and gain a confidence and perspective that we can then bring to larger public discussion. Congregations can build capacity for the difficult conversations so needed in recultivating civic engagement.

An Invitation to Difficult Conversations

The convocation at the seminary where I teach was not an isolated incident. At the lunch table, in classes, in conversations with one

9

another and with teachers, the students had learned to tiptoe around the issues that might be controversial, painful, or unresolved. This behavior went far beyond "political correctness" to a noticeable avoidance of conflict and risk. Passions were buried. Theological institutions such as ours have had a rich history of robust debate. As much education could be absorbed in late-night bull sessions as in listening to carefully crafted lectures. The oral history of seminaries often contains colorful stories of famous "conversations." Yet those who would be the next generation of church leaders were not learning these skills. In fact, they were learning how to avoid them, how to remain disengaged.

In true academic form, the seminary faculty assumed that for any problem there must be a curricular solution. A course was created to begin at least to address the problem. It was titled "The Church and the World," but students quickly dubbed it "Difficult Conversations." The purpose of the course from its inception has been to establish the format and to provide a safe place for students to wade into difficult subjects. Lectures introduce issues that are at once personal and political—but all of them tough. Students are then encouraged to try out new language and risk exploring their perspectives in small groups and in journals. That course, first taught in 1996, provided the inspiration for this book. It remains one of my most profound, mutually transformative teaching experiences. In fact, since it is counterintuitive for an individual to write in isolation about conversation, this project is something of a collective effort. Members of that first class worked with me on the idea for the book and have given input throughout. In other words, the book you now hold is the product of many conversations—some very difficult!

But this is a book primarily for

congregations. Little direction will be given on the content of the conversations in which a congregation might engage, as there was with the class. The material for your conversations is yours to identify. Certainly you will find enough grist to sustain rich conversation indefinitely. This book instead invites you into a process that I hope will be habit-forming. Difficult conversations, at best, are not relegated to a committee, a program, or a course, although that is where they might begin. Rather, I am proposing a new way of being church as a community where even the most difficult issues can be energetically engaged among the gathered and, ultimately, in the public forum.

In the next chapter I begin an examination of why congregations have not been contexts that have engendered difficult conversation. What dynamics are at work that enable committed and caring believers so effectively to silence one another? Chapter 3 considers the most basic element in difficult conversations—risk. But risk in this context does not emerge from personal strength and moral clarity. The courage to risk is drawn largely from the trust and support of conversation partners. Only then can it become a creative process rather than a single event in time. Chapter 4 explores models of cultivating difficult conversations, drawn from the experiences of congregations. Chapter 5 asks, "What's the Point?" A wise preaching professor encouraged me to organize sermons around the question "So what?" Where does all this lead? Is conversation an end in itself? Finally, how does difficult conversation become a sustained and healthy part of a congregation's culture and dynamics? If not cultivated, fruitful conversation will not happen by itself.

Questions for Discussion

1. Think about all the places where conversations occur in your congregation—at coffee hour, in meetings, in Sunday school, on retreats, in the parking lot.

- What are some of the major themes in these conversations?
- What types of conversation are more likely to occur in different contexts?

2. Are there any taboo topics? Can you think of any issues or particular positions on issues that would not be tolerated within the congregation?

- Why do you think these conversational topics cannot be discussed?
- If you wanted to have a conversation about one of these subjects, where or with whom might you have it?

3. Think about an awkward moment in a conversation, either personal or public. What made it uncomfortable for you?

CHAPTER 2

What Makes Difficult Conversations So Difficult?

I have a large file in my memory bank that I have labeled my "cringe file." Any of the events in this mental portfolio can make me cringe— even the image of a moment long ago that dimly races across my consciousness. Mostly the file holds memories of conflicts and difficult conversations that were painful to move through. Some were never resolved; some are conversations that never happened but should have. Although I am far from being a psychologist or pastoral counselor, my hunch is that most of us have some cringe-producing recollections: breaking up with someone special, confronting a friend, "coming out," admitting a failure. These are relegated to a place in our memories different from that where conflicts we have had with institutions or strangers reside. While our inadequacies here can also make us wince in recollection, the regret or embarrassment we carry toward those whom we don't know does not match the degree of cringing conjured up by a failure in one of our more intimate relationships.

Conversations become much more difficult when we are in dialogue with one who matters deeply to us. Even if we feel angry or alienated from a friend or family member, we care about the direction of the conver-sation and the impact of our words. We are concerned about how we present ourselves and how we are perceived. We have a lot at stake in these conversations. Will the risk be worth it? Will the relationship be transformed in ways we hope for? Will we be rejected? How much are we willing to change in our perceptions, language, and position without compromising our own integrity?

Difficult conversations occupy a separate space in our lives. We do not, nor could we, live entirely in this realm. They require much more energy than everyday conversation because they carry multiple levels of meaning that go well below the words spoken, to the core of our own identities. They bring to the surface fundamental questions we have about ourselves: Am I a good person? A fair person? A person of faith? Do I have courage? Am I being true to myself? We wade into difficult conversations carefully, measuring our words and trying to listen to the voice of our inner self and perhaps to God.

No wonder, then, that we want to minimize the need for difficult conversations and have developed elaborate strategies to avoid them. In our personal lives we might ignore a conflict or move away from a relationship where we see such a conversation brewing. In our communities of faith we do the same things. The cost, in both cases, is that by avoiding the conversations we know will be difficult, we also sacrifice the opportunity for growth, a clearer sense of who we are, and a more honest basis for relationship. Of course, to get to the true conversation, we need both intention and skill. A conversation marked by honesty, trust, mutual respect, civility, and openness to new ideas will be no less difficult, but more satisfying. In our better moments, we know this to be true.

These values are not just personal or even cultural, however; they represent theological convictions as well. We would hope to see these same virtues in our congregations. When we think about who we are as a people of God, we hope that within our life together we have the capacity for *respecting one another.* Standing together as we do each week before the God who both judges and forgives, we expect that there could be among us the possibility for *humility and honesty.* Understanding that the church is bound with sacred ties, we imagine that we might be a *trusting community.* Affirming the ongoing creation of God and the work of the Holy Spirit (who like the wind, after all, blows where it will), we assume that people of faith should especially be *open to new ideas.* In other words, of all people

in society we hope that *especially* those who gather as communities of faith should be capable of cultivating and sustaining difficult conversations. After all, if not here, then where? What better context is there than our churches, temples, and synagogues in which to struggle through the most difficult issues in our society? We believe of ourselves that, by the grace of God, we have access to important spiritual and cultural resources to bring to the task of engaging in difficult conversations.

As is so often the case, the ideal image of what *should be* clouds our vision of what actually *is.* Although in congregations we regularly confess our shortcomings together, that does not mean that we are free from romantic ideas about who we are. As theologians we can be long on prescriptive thinking and fall short on the descriptive task of understanding the current reality.

15

Yet whether witnessing vicious denominational battles over homosexuality, resulting in rigid standoffs or threats of schism, or being given the cold shoulder at a Sunday morning coffee hour, we know that our religious gatherings fall far short of our potential for engaging in sustained difficult conversations. To understand why we might go to such lengths to avoid difficult conversation, it is sometimes easier to peek into a congregation other than our own.

An Experiment in Difficult Conversation

During the 1960s, racial tensions were running high throughout the United States. The civil rights movement had challenged Americans on entrenched racism, thereby creating the agenda for perhaps the most difficult of national conversations.

Martin Luther King, Jr., and other activists valued the role of public dialogue in moving toward the goal of positive social and political change. Others were less patient, expressing the understandable accumulated rage of generations of oppression and broken promises.

Many within the religious sector participated in the multifaceted social movement for racial justice. The images of King marching arm in arm with black and white religious leaders across the ecumenical spectrum are ingrained in our cultural memory. Predominantly white denominations articulated bold, unprecedented statements condemning racism as sinful at personal and institutional levels. One Protestant denomination based in the Midwest decided to show its congregations how they could become involved in the struggle for civil rights.

The strategy was elegantly simple. A typical congregation was chosen: Augustana Lutheran Church in Omaha, Nebraska. A relatively large, white, middle-class church in a midsize city, it had begun struggling with racial issues. Leaders in the black churches and the community at large were organizing. The mayor was responding to charges of racism in Omaha by denouncing the injustice experienced by returning black Vietnam veterans who found that adequate housing and well-paying jobs were unavailable to them in their own hometown. Many of the veterans lived in segregated neighborhoods not far from Augustana Church.

The denomination decided to appoint one of its brightest and best, the Rev. Bill Youngdahl, as the new pastor. He would lead the congregation's members through difficult conversations around race with one another and with their neighbors. While movie cameras recorded the process, the congrega-

tion would, it was hoped, be transformed and become an agent of change in the city. The resulting film would inspire other congregations to engage in such conversations. For months, the cameras rolled during committee meetings, worship, adult forums, Sunday school classes, and the pastor's conversations with local clergy and black leaders in a local barbershop. (This era predated the technology of voyeuristic TV; those filmed in the documentary had to accommodate the presence of the technician, the whir of the camera, and the glare of bright lights. Even so, the film provides some of the best footage of a real congregation at work being a congregation, given that the genre itself is limited.)

Youngdahl's strategy was modest from the perspective of the 21st century. After a youth-group exchange with a black Presbyterian church close by, the pastor proposed family exchanges between the two congregations. Ten volunteer families from each church would meet in each other's homes for a meal and conversation. Conflict mounted in the congregation in a drama more riveting than any found in today's voyeuristic TV shows. To their credit, Augustana members allowed the cameras to keep filming throughout their struggle. Finally Pastor Youngdahl felt pressured to resign after just one year in the Omaha pastorate. At the end of the film, *A Time for Burning*,[1] he is seen hanging up his alb and stole and walking out of the church as the folksinger Ronnie Gilbert sings of a future time when justice might prevail.

Looking back, it is easy for contemporary viewers to feel smug about how far our culture has evolved in the past 35 years. In the film, many people are smokers. The gas-guzzling cars look like clunkers or classics, depending on one's perspective. Women are passive and

obviously absent from the decision-making structures of the church. Clothing styles look out of date, and women wear "cat's-eye" glasses. And of course, who would balk today at a simple act of hospitality between the members of two mainline Protestant churches? But some things don't change—including the message that is preached about racial reconciliation and the reasons congregations have for avoiding difficult conversations.

Many church leaders insist throughout the film that although they agree with the goals of racial justice, the step proposed is a threat to the unity and perhaps even the survival of the church. The words "The time is not good" become a litany repeated throughout the deliberations. For the members of Augustana, institutional survival is of utmost importance. They don't think that talk is cheap—in fact, in this context it is considered downright inflammatory and it threatens to divide them. To preserve the unity and harmony of our "bonded" networks (families, schools, associations, churches), most people avoid the "bridging" activity of conversations that could be difficult—those that introduce a different perspective or issue a challenge. In some part of our institutional consciousness, we do believe that sticks and stones could break our bones—and so could words.

After Youngdahl resigned, those who had silently supported his proposals regretted that they had not come to his defense. They had not entered into the difficult conversations within and about the church because they did not trust their own voices. Many were women who had been relegated to the sidelines of church politics and had developed a sense of inferiority. Although women are much more strongly present in congregational leadership today, many people in our communities of faith—men as well as women—still do not trust their voices enough to engage in difficult conversation. Often they do not feel confident of their grasp of biblical and theological concepts and language. Perhaps they think they do not know enough about an issue. Surely "the experts" know much more and can resolve the issue (an enormous leap of faith). Many people believe that their voices would be insignificant—so why bother?

Those at Augustana and in our own congregations opt out of difficult conversations for other reasons. Remaining silent is the best defense against rejection. Cultures develop intricate and subterranean mechanisms for censure—for making sure that dissenting voices are muffled or even punished. While most religious groups would be appalled at the Amish practice of shunning, we shun in more subtle ways those

19

who would articulate an unpopular or unacceptable position. Being "frozen out" of a group can feel to the victim as cruel as any "defrocking" or "disciplinary action." Even if confident in our position and comfortable with our voice, we risk rejection if we speak out.

"Do you feel your pastor is preaching the truth?" a local black leader challenged representatives of Augustana. After they numbly nodded in the affirmative, he pressed them further. "Then obviously you support him and expect him to be here for a long time, right?" He knew the dynamics of avoiding the difficult conversation of race within the church as well as outside its walls. He could also have prophesied that the risk the courageous pastor had taken would result in rejection.

Not all members of Augustana maintained a pattern of avoidance, however. The head of the social outreach committee consistently took risks to engage others in discussions outside his experience and comfort zone. He risked appearing unenlightened or even racist when talking with African American clergy and civil rights leaders. He risked appearing disloyal as he quietly pursued the issue within his congregation. While often challenged on the ideas he was forming, he was not afraid to explore questions that remained unresolved in his mind. He represented the seeds of change that eventually helped to move the congregation intact through social change.

A Time for Burning does not represent a "bad" congregation, but one brimming with all the humanity characteristic of every community of faith. We might intuitively know where we need to go and that we must move through uncharted waters to get there. We also have strong preservationist instincts. We want to protect both the unity of our church and our membership in it. The problem is that we make subconscious assumptions in our protective avoidance—assumptions about ourselves, the "unity" that exists, and the danger of conversation. We want to avoid those dangerous conversations that might challenge and, worse, *change* us. And we devise strategies for making sure these discussions don't happen.

Constructing Strategies of Avoidance

The exceptional few thrive on conflict. In some cases, they are admired for their courage, romanticized as heroic figures of uncommon character taking a stand as individuals, stemming the tide of popular opinion and institutional strength because "I can do no other." Usually, however, these heat-seeking conversation partners are not regarded

in such glowing terms. Because they ask impertinent questions, they are perceived as "troublemakers," "pot-stirrers," "agitators." They transgress the understood limits of how honest we should be, and can kill a committee meeting or dampen a party.

Most of us, however, or most of us most of the time, do not engage in such socially risky behavior. We would rather avoid conflict (sometimes at all costs), as well as the difficult conversations that could lead to conflict or make us feel that we're already embroiled in it. In congregations, as in families and at the workplace, we develop strategies for avoiding such conversations. A few strategies have been uncloseted above, but their name is legion.

Congregational cultures, like other social networks, gravitate to the lowest common denominator in conversation. Although we are drawn together around the mysteries of the

21

universe to make meaning of our deepest questions and experiences—birth, relationship, vocation, community, sinfulness, and death—our conversation focuses on the shared concerns and certainties of daily life. And so, a woman struggling with an unwanted pregnancy may talk about the weather at coffee hour rather than about the subject that consumes her thoughts. Our country may be threatening to go to war, but we talk about the Sunday school schedule. Our state is going to execute its first prisoner in ten years, but at the committee meeting we talk about our children's summer camps. The community is divided on whether the planned Ku Klux Klan march is an expression of racial aggression or free speech, but the church is preoccupied with its capital campaign. An anthropologist might be surprised to analyze the content of conversation in and around communities of faith. It can be surprisingly superficial and mundane —indistinguishable from country-club conviviality or grocery-store small talk.

Such everyday conversation can serve two purposes. The first is constructive: such talk represents the basic human connection that is the glue of any social network. Here, relationships are made and reinforced. Mutual concern may be expressed and a sense of belonging experienced by those who converse. Social capital is generated, and in Robert Putnam's categories, it is of the bonding type.[2] Our community life is strengthened, at least at a surface level. We're reminding each other of who we are and reminding ourselves that we are part of this group. Bonding, in itself, is not a bad thing—unless it undermines social connections that build bridges across communities. Social *bonding* fulfills an important human need.

But social *bridging* is critical to human survival and progress.

The second purpose served in that common-denominator conversation is less constructive: it undermines the possibility that difficult conversations will happen. It both brings about the bonding of the group and limits the depth of bonding. It does so in three ways:

- By simply filling up the airtime
- By communicating that only topics on which we agree on can be introduced
- By communicating that issues not on the agenda are therefore not important

This strategy is effective in deflecting potential conflict for long periods of time. But it stems from misguided notions about institutional survival. As Nancy Ammerman has shown in her research on congregations, the congregations in

"changing neighborhoods" that flee potential conflict by relocating the church, or that stay and "circle the wagons" do not experience the vitality and growth of churches that are open to conflict.

Sometimes, as at First Congregational and First Existentialist, conflict is simply assumed. It comes and goes, forming and re-forming around various issues, but not threatening the stability of the congregation in any significant way. These highly educated, highly participatory people expect to disagree with one another. There are strong democratic traditions in these congregations and democracy does not mean, for them, routine unanimous votes. Occasionally someone gets unhappy enough to leave, but even that is seen as the natural outgrowth of persons finding their own best place to worship (or

23

not worship). These are friendly divorces, not acrimonious ones. . . . This pattern of conflict . . . stands in remarkable contrast to the peacefulness of the declining (in membership), moving (relocating) and niche (specific ministry) congregations.[3]

Other strategies can be employed to keep difficult issues at arm's length. In fact, these strategies may be more effective because they give the congregation the impression that it *is* wrestling with issues. For example, rather than just talking about family events and the last movie we saw, we focus our conversation on the Bible, theology, and the life of faith. But we do this in such a way that we relegate the discussion to a spiritual realm, far removed from the complex and unresolved nitty-gritty issues that gnaw at us. Even when we can "take to the Lord in prayer" our struggles over

removing our children from a troubled school or staying and trying to change it—we may not feel that we can take it to the *Lord's people* in discussion to help us in our discernment. After all, John is on the school board, Judy is home-schooling her children, and the Ricardos have little Ricky in an exclusive private school. Passions about family decisions run strong, and the risk of offending a family or appearing to be an unconcerned citizen or an inadequate parent is too great. Better that we just talk about Jesus' invitation for children to come to him in Sunday school, and pray for children *en masse* in the liturgy. The result is that an important resource in our decision-making—the collective wisdom of the community of faith—is unavailable not only for parents in the congregation, but for the community at large as well.

Sometimes churches do decide to "take on an issue." But they ensure that it does not become an occasion for the hard work of wrestling with complex issues in light of multiple social realities and faith perspectives. Out of a commitment to fairness and tolerance, we organize educational forums in which "all sides can be presented," often on separate weeks. The hope is that church members, armed with enough information on the topic, can then clarify their own positions and act on them as individual citizens. We further hope that this educational process will be enough to contribute to the common good. Certainly this model, best exemplified by the League of Women Voters, fills an important role in a democracy. But providing information is but one component in education, as any teacher knows. Real education happens as participants engage in dialogue, bringing different life experiences and theological viewpoints to bear. Education is a process, often an uncomfortable one, of moving through difficult conversation and debate. It is not simply an event. The organizing committee cannot predict the outcome—and for many church education committees, that's scary.

When planning such an educational series or process, another strategy is to make the issue as abstract as possible. Depersonalizing issues for discussion in congregations provides a higher level of common denominator but installs a "glass floor" that prevents us from bringing to the discussion the messiness of everyday life. In sermons, classes, small-group discussions, and Bible studies we might be so bold as to put homosexuality on the agenda. But the issue is discussed in such broad strokes that the confused parents who suspect that their son is gay, or the teenager trying to make sense of her sexual identity, cannot bring their lived realities into the conversation. The lesbian on the church board feels invisible in such discussions—and in

25

fact she has been made to be, so that the issue can be discussed without conflict.

Conversation is the most basic unit of social capital. In a complex, pluralistic society it is inevitable that many of the conversations that need to happen will be difficult if we are to move toward some resolution, even one short of consensus. The loss of the will or the skill of difficult conversation can have serious implications for a democratic society. To understand the decline of social capital, perhaps a starting place is to look at our increasing reluctance to leave private comfort zones to encounter others who represent different perspectives, values, and experience.

Within faith communities, which provide both affinity and support, this trend is especially troubling. By engaging in avoidance of potential conflict, we undermine the possibilities of creativity, vitality, and change. We also demonstrate that we do not truly endorse two primary faith commitments—trust in the work of the Holy Spirit and in the sisters and brothers who make up our community of faith. Engaging in difficult conversations will mean that we must risk such trust.

Questions for Discussion

1. Suppose your pastor suggested a program of mutual visitation among households of two different churches as Pastor Youngdahl did at Augustana Church. Perhaps instead of an exchange that involves a congregation made up primarily of those of a different racial or religious background, the proposal involves a congregation with openly gay and lesbian members.

- How might your congregation respond?
- What would be some of its fears?

2. Some strategies for avoiding difficult conversations were identified in this chapter— engaging in small talk, speaking of issues in abstract or spiritual terms, sponsoring forums for gathering information but not directly engaging different perspectives.

- Which of these strategies have you experienced in your own congregation?
- In your experience, by what other means are difficult conversations avoided?

CHAPTER 3

Emergent Trust and Transformative Risk

I n the modern classic *The Lives of a Cell,* Lewis Thomas, a biologist and astute social observer, described the dynamic interaction of all living things on our planet as one giant cell. Insects, trees, people, fish, birds, flowers—the entire ecosystem—develop and sustain an interdependence that keeps the whole thing living and growing. Humanity engages with the whole and with each other, the encounters themselves forming a kind of glue. That is to say, we humans organize ourselves through systems of give and take, forming a dynamic nucleus of the cell—although we can never be independent of the rest of the cell. Even though Thomas was not a social scientist, the metaphor remains as compelling and poetic as it is idealistic. What he described in organic terms as being essential to life is what sociologists call social capital. A decline in social capital, as documented by Robert Putnam *(Bowling Alone)* and others, could have devastating consequences for the very survival of the whole cell. When dynamic interaction slacks off, the social cell comes unglued.

Looking through a social microscope, let's probe deeper to try to understand this buzzing connectedness. If, as was asserted in the previous chapter, conversation is the most basic unit of social capital, then what is its DNA? What makes the connection we call conversation happen at all? What are the basic elements and the essential conditions that might make difficult conversations possible?

Many factors may prompt a conversation. A person may be lonely or curious, need information or resources, desire to celebrate good news or share bad, seek reinforcement for his or her values, or want to challenge those of another. We have a myriad of motives for entering into all kinds of conversation, but always there is a primary assumption of *trust*. I trust that you will listen or have the information I need. I trust that you will respond and not walk away. I trust that I will not be ignored or attacked. I trust that I know generally where you're coming from. Without some level of trust, conversation is not possible. It is the primary precondition for this most basic form of social exchange.

Putnam distinguishes between "thin" and "thick" trust.[1] "Thick trust" is built up over time between people who have come to know one another. Whether in relationship with an intimate partner, colleague, teacher, or a person one only sees on a regular basis in the community, our experience with the other gives us some sense that we can predict a response. "Thin trust" is what we extend to strangers. We trust other drivers to stop at a red light, for example. As we move through society and barter or banter with those we don't know, we act out of an assumption of trust. Trust is reciprocated and extended to us as well. However thin, this type of trust makes life together possible, moving us from a collection of independent individuals to a functional community of strangers.

In communities of faith, both types of trust are present and necessary. The thick trust of experience forges the bonds of congregational life. Familiar folk surround us in worship, sitting in predictable locations. We may not know their names (and may be well beyond the time that we would have felt comfortable asking) but still we feel that we know these people. We trust them enough to ask for prayer to be offered for the struggles of life. The pastor acts in trust each week in initiating dialogue through the sermon. We trust one another enough to sing, speak, and maybe even clap, and risk looking foolish. We talk at coffee hour. All of this communication does not have to be based on a network of close relationships (although that is also present); but it does rest on a foundation of thick trust.

Trust is then extended to those unknown to us outside the walls of the congregation in the wider faith community. It is *thin trust* that becomes the essential tendon holding ecumenical organizations and denominational families together. Although the members of our Episcopal parish in Detroit do not know the Episcopalians in North Carolina, there is reciprocal trust in our shared experience and commitment that makes it possible for us to claim one religious identity and to support one institution that can survive the upheavals of history. Presbyterians in an Atlanta church may not know the members of Baptist and Lutheran churches nearby but have enough mutual trust to begin an ecumenical dialogue.

Even as social trust is essential for a society, it has been the lifeblood of the church since its very beginning. The apostle Paul often conversed by letter with the emerging church, and at points many of these conversations became difficult.

From the beginning of his letters, it is apparent that Paul is speaking to some with whom he has had intense relationships and many more whom he has never met. Both thin and thick trust undergird Paul's communication.

> Paul and Timothy, servants of
> Christ Jesus,
> To all the saints in Christ Jesus
> who are in Philippi, with
> the bishops and deacons:
> Grace to you and peace from
> God our Father and the
> Lord Jesus Christ.
> I thank my God every time I
> remember you (Phil. 1:1-3).

The thick trust that results from more intimate communication is not a superior form. Both types are essential components of social capital and all the conversations that contribute to it. For communities of faith to survive and thrive, as with community in general, both kinds of social trust are essential.

However, according to Robert Putnam's indicators, about the same time that social capital started to decline (in the last 30 to 40 years), social trust began ebbing as well.[2] Drawing from highly reputable survey samples, he found that in 1960 more than half of Americans affirmed that "Most people can be trusted," rather than "You can't be too careful in dealing with people." However, by the end of the century only one-third were trusting and two-thirds operated out of social suspicion rather than trust. When broken down by generation, it was clear that each succeeding generation was less trusting than the previous one. Generations did not change their perspectives over time but remained remarkably consistent. Therefore, as the most trusting generation (born before 1930) fades from society, it is being replaced by less trusting ones (those born after 1960).

Beyond survey data, other indications tell us that even our thin trust has worn thinner. Compliance with the census was once considered a civic no-brainer. Now census takers are met with resistance and sometimes contempt. Road rage is on the rise, and hitchhiking is now rarely seen. Crime is decreasing, but employment in security and law enforcement has soared since 1970.[3] Urban residents speak nostalgically about the days when they could spend summer evenings sitting on the porch. The fear of crime keeps air conditioners running and urbanites inside—not only off the porch but reluctant to go out for evening activities, as most parish clergy know already. First graders are no longer taught to duck and cover in case of nuclear attack but how to "drop and run," should a stranger approach them.

The connection between social trust and social capital becomes apparent. With a declining sense of comfort among the populace, people have an incentive to disengage. Casting a wary eye toward those we don't know, we are less willing to join organizations, attend a community meeting, canvass for a candidate, or trust that dollars sent to those who do engage in such activities will be well spent. Perhaps it is because we don't join and participate that social trust has begun to atrophy.

A number of explanations suggest why this trend toward social disengagement is happening now. Several hypotheses have emerged that attempt to explain the decline in social trust and social capital—media, technology, increased social distance between rich and poor, for example. It is not even clear whether the decline in trust is an outcome or the cause of declining social capital. Even Robert Putnam cannot sort out cause and effect. What is clear is that the civic atmosphere—and the broader social context in which religious communities are embedded—is less trusting now than it was 50 or even 30 years ago. The slow evaporation of social trust puts difficult conversations, or any type of conversation, on an endangered list.

Social Trust in the Company of the Committed

But how about the church—are our members less trusting now than they were a generation ago? Is thin and thick trust declining in our congregations, denominations, and ecumenical groups? Certainly we are very much part of our cultural context. Yet doesn't the community of faith bring particular resources that are uniquely suited to build trust? We articulate a common worldview in the shared language of our liturgies. We affirm both our diversity and a unity that transcends it. We acknowledge a shared belief that before God, all have sinned and all are loved. In Christian communions, the metaphor of the body—requiring the interdependence of all the various parts—is a celebrated image of the church itself. We worship a God who we believe binds us together in ways we cannot understand. Surely these rich resources of spirit and identity should not only resist the erosion of trust in our communities of faith, but nurture that trust.

It is hard to measure trust specifically in our religious groupings. But looking at the ways people of faith differ from or reflect the population at large will give us a glimpse of our "trust barometer."

- Data show a relationship between the concurrent trends of declining social trust and social participation. Similar patterns are evident in the church. While the well-documented decline in church membership from 1960 to the present has begun to plateau, church attendance and involvement in church-related activities have fallen more dramatically. Membership among all church groups fell 10 percent in the last four decades, but participation is off by 25 percent to 50 percent.[4] Assuming that the same patterns are at work among religious people as in the culture at large, less face-to-face interaction means lower levels of the "thin" trust so critical for the maintenance of community.

- Although the religious sector accounts for half of all charitable giving in the country, a marked decline in contributions is seen across the ecumenical spectrum. Americans have been significantly less generous to church and charity alike in the last 15 years, even amid economic prosperity. More troubling is the fact that among Protestants, giving to others ("benevolences") has fallen more than three times faster than the declining contribution to ourselves (church finances).[5] Catholics have experienced an even steeper drop in contributions, falling 59 percent between 1960 and 1989. If treasure follows the heart, indications are that our hearts are not as strongly attached to our faith communities as they once were.

Is trust in our brothers and sisters in the faith declining? In some ways we are indistinguishable from the culture at large: we're less generous with our money and less active in our participation than we were four decades ago. It is probably safe to assume that people of faith follow

35

the same pattern of declining social trust as well. Yet it is impossible to tease out the chicken-and-egg sequence between social trust and social connectedness. Are we withdrawing from church and synagogue life because trust is waning, or does trust recede because we simply don't have as much opportunity to get together and build trusting relationships? Probably the two trends reinforce each other—but the result is the same. With declining trust the difficult conversations so badly needed to move us to some consensus and healing around divisive issues are less likely to occur. Again the question compels our attention: "If not in the community of faith, then where can such conversations take place?"

There is some evidence that the religious sector is using its resources to recultivate trust and conversation. Putnam presents data showing that religious participants are more likely to join other clubs and to donate blood than are those who are not part of a faith community. In fact, as church activity increases, so does participation in other organizations.[6] In other words, when looking at where social connections are being made, we see a consistent link with religious participation. As any sociologist worth her salt will remind you, correlations don't really explain anything. We cannot tell from this information whether joining clubs prompts church attendance or vice versa. But it is clear that people of faith are joiners. Religion has not become hopelessly privatized or reinvented by electronic or virtual churches. Faith still has the capacity to draw us together in both "bonding" and "bridging" activity.

Whom Do You Trust?

Trust is indeed a precious commodity—an increasingly rare yet essential precondition for any social interaction. But what is trust? While our first association might be affective, clearly trust is not a warm fuzzy feeling that can be conjured up or constructed as needed. Anyone who has been a parent knows that it is possible to have tender feelings for those whom you cannot always trust. Trust is a confidence in other people or even in institutions that they will act with integrity and in ways that are constructive (or at least not destructive). It is an expectation built on experience—an informed hope. Those who have lived with an alcoholic know how important trust is in restoring a relationship. But even though trust might be longed for, it must be earned. A loving partner cannot sustain trust unless promises are kept. Building trust can be hard work. We cannot build it in isolation, by ourselves, but only in relationship.

It is understandable that without ongoing relationships with others, individuals find it increasingly hard to find a basis for trust. But mistrust feeds disengagement, just as disengagement results in a lack of social trust. So it is hard to know where to jump in to change the cycle.

Our loss of trust in religious institutions is understandable. Seedy scandals have put religion on the nightly news. Embezzlements, sexual harassment and exploitation cases, and stories of other misuses of spiritual power have rocked the church and chipped away at the social trust needed to keep communities of faith together and strong. How can trust in the integrity of our religious institutions be restored? We cannot simply pray that a feeling of confidence will return.

Sociological data and common sense tell us that trust happens when people are brought together and given the opportunity to engage each other. Difficult conversations are more likely to occur with more social contacts, and can produce more social trust, which consequently engenders more social engagement. It takes some social trust, of course, to participate in a religious community at all. But in social encounter, some of it hard, we learn to trust more and go to deeper levels of conversation. Just as trust cannot be reduced to a feeling, so it must not be seen as a single entity that you either have or don't have. Creating social trust—thick or thin—is a process that builds its own momentum.

A few years ago I was involved in a study of "renewing congregations" conducted by the seminary at which I teach. My colleagues and I studied Christian congregations from a variety of theological traditions. What they had in common was that each of these local churches had been dramatically renewed in their identity, mission, and vitality. (This renewal did not always mean numerical growth, by the way.) We were looking for the secret ingredient, the magic bullet. We hoped that by identifying the variable that explained congregational vitality we could better equip our students to lead congregations through renewal. What we found, of course, was much more complex. The renewing churches had employed all kinds of strategies, leadership models, and theological perspectives. There was no magic bullet that would fit neatly into our program.

But there was one point of consistency. Every congregation, in telling its story, pointed to a moment of risk on which the narrative turned. At some point, an individual or group of people had taken a chance on a new way of "doing church" or a new way of looking at faith. Sometimes it was the minister or priest who had proposed a new approach to worship or program. At other times a group of people within the church had taken a chance in changing the direction of the congregation, in most cases by reorienting themselves to those outside the congregation. At the time, the risks had seemed radical and had created tension in the congregation. Usually dissenters worried aloud that the programs could fail or divide the church. By definition, a risk would not be risky if the possibility of failure and conflict were not present. Usually, the risks did provoke some level of conflict, and heated negotiations ensued. But in retrospect, the risks and conflicts proved to be a pivotal point in the congregation's development.

Some level of social trust had to be in play already for the risk-taker to take the plunge. The whole process of revitalization required a series of risks and conflicts—some smaller, others more dramatic. But at each point, for the risk to be taken, trust had to be tested and built, brick by brick, conversation by conversation. Social capital was being generated as struggles over identity and resources meant that folk had to get off the bench and into the huddle.

Risk and trust are mutually reinforcing elements in the DNA of difficult conversations. As loving as our fellowship may seem, or as civil as our congregational dynamics may be, engaging in difficult conversations is risky business. It raises in our minds the question "Just how much do we trust each other?" Of course, stepping out in faith can generate trust we never knew was there. Demonstrating honesty, curiosity, and acceptance invites conversation partners to reciprocate. Social trust can be created as conversation is risked. Such conversations can be transformative for congregations. But how do risk and trust result in change?

Risking Change

Jesus was a unique conversation partner—at times obscure, at other times direct. He could speak at length, offer only cryptic messages, or remain silent. As maddening or confusing as he could be in some conversations, he remained trustworthy and compelling. Many of his conversations have survived history because they were memorable and transformative. One such encounter was with a Canaanite woman (Matt. 15:21-28, Mark 7:24-30).

Here, Jesus was drawn into conversation across enormous social distance. Talking with a member of her ethnic group, and moreover a woman, broke social convention. Seemingly, Jesus was initially quite willing to honor these boundaries. In Mark's account, the woman found Jesus hiding in a house. Matthew records him as being on the road with his disciples, who strongly advised him not to talk to her. In both cases, Jesus clearly was resistant to engaging the woman. The conversation was a result of risk-taking on her part. She was consumed by a personal struggle, one not normally spoken of in polite company: her daughter was "tormented by a demon," according to Matthew's telling. Yet the one who is known for his compassion told her that his mission was to the House of Israel. He actively withdrew from conversation with her. To drive his point home, he said that helping one of her people would be like throwing his children's food to the dogs. In essence he was saying that his children deserved to be fed, but hers did not.

Persistent even in the face of a racial slur, the woman did not react but stayed on topic. "Even the dogs under the table eat the children's crumbs." Her cool-headed tenacity, the risk she took, and the trust in Jesus' healing power paid off.

The conversation had been awkward and tense, but finally transformed both of them. "'For saying that, you may go—the demon has left your daughter.' So she went home, found the child lying on the bed, and the demon was gone" (Mark 7:29-30). After 2,000 years, that conversation continues to challenge and change those who read the story.

Still, we know that the easy part of difficult conversations is avoiding them. We duck into our house to hide from the public. We tell ourselves and each other not to bring up certain topics and not to talk to certain people. Sometimes we're even nasty about it. The tactics for thwarting social trust and social capital are as old as sin.

But there are still some Canaanite women out there who go against the social tide: congregations that, in a variety of ways and on a variety of topics, are taking risks to initiate difficult conversations and to create safe places where the talk can be sustained. We turn now to look more closely at those communities of faith where risk and trust beget change.

Questions for Discussion

1. Robert Putnam demonstrates that in the last 30 years, congregations have experienced lower levels of participation in activities and per-capita giving, even when membership has stayed the same or even increased.

- What have been the trends in membership, attendance, participation, and giving in your own congregation?
- What groups or activities have experienced a loss of participation?
- Which have seen more participation? Why?

2. How would you describe the levels of thin and thick trust in your church? For example, would you feel comfortable enough to

- welcome someone to worship whom you don't know?
- join a committee or go to an activity where you did not know anyone?
- sing a solo in church?
- ask for prayer or pray aloud with another member?
- talk to someone in your church about doubts you have?
- speak against a popular motion in a meeting?
- talk to another member about how much money you should give to the church?

3. Think about your own congregation's history. When have you seen "turning points"? What was going on at those times—what risks were being taken?

CHAPTER 4

Cultivating Difficult Conversations

For most North Americans, it is hard to appreciate fully what April 27, 1994, meant for South Africans. On that day the cruel system of racial apartheid officially ended as the majority population in that country was able to vote for the first time. Almost in disbelief, people of color lined up at the polls and elected Nelson Mandela to be the first post-apartheid president. As a revered black leader, Mandela had never wavered in his commitment to democracy—despite having spent 28 years in the brutal prison conditions of Robben Island, including extended periods of solitary confinement.

He was but a single, albeit symbolic, victim of a system that had for nearly five decades oppressed the overwhelming majority of black and racially mixed South Africans. Blacks were forced to live in impoverished "townships." The inferior public education they received all but ensured that dreams would be aborted, young minds left undeveloped, and young people prepared only for work in the diamond mines or the kitchens of white families. Families were separated as parents traveled to their jobs

43

outside the townships. If caught without an identification pass, a black South African was at the mercy of the South African police, who were not known for their just treatment of those in their custody. Human rights were flouted as books, ideas, music, and even people were banned. Organized peaceful protest could be deadly, even when the dissenters were only children (as in Soweto when children were shot for protesting the use of the Afrikaans language in their instruction). Suspected leaders of the opposition were jailed and tortured; sometimes they disappeared altogether. Violence begat violence, and factions within the opposition movement began to battle each other. As the world watched the horror of apartheid continue, an increasingly isolated South Africa appeared to be on a bloody trajectory. Despite global peacemaking efforts—including those of the churches—it was hard to imagine a resolution that was not apocalyptic. If God did not intervene, the South African juggernaut was hurtling toward a final battle that would leave few survivors.

Even after the miraculous negotiated transition, which resulted in the election of Mandela, it was hard to imagine that years of accumulated righteous rage would not find violent expression. How could the newly freed black majority not seek revenge once in power? Could South Africans of all colors possibly form a viable and united nation?

Historically two models presented themselves at this stage in nation building. In post-Holocaust Europe a future in which such atrocities would "never again" be a reality was considered possible only if those involved in the Nazi system were brought to justice. Beginning at Nuremberg and continuing to the present day, "war criminals" have been tracked down, tried, and punished. Although the resulting sense of closure can never compensate for the loss of millions of victims, such retributive justice does provide some catharsis for survivors. Still, the wound is never fully healed.

In other contexts war-weary countries have decided to look only toward the future and to bury the past. In a few Latin American countries, for example, a general amnesty has been declared, covering all past offenses committed in the context of war. While past pain does not have to be publicly relived, the truth is never fully known and justice is denied. Again, the wounds of the victims continue to bleed.

Either of these strategies toward reconciliation would have been understandable in the South African context. But the reforming nation chose neither to deny the past nor to seek vengeance for it. The new leaders realized that they could not ignore the suffering of so many people. To Anglican Archbishop Desmond Tutu, amnesty constituted a policy of amnesia and would, in effect, "victimize the victims of apartheid a second time around."[1] Pursuit of legal accountability through a judicial system thoroughly corrupted by apartheid was also discounted. Besides, the people of South Africa needed to get about the business of living together as one nation. "We have had to balance the requirements of justice, accountability, stability, peace and reconciliation,"[2] Tutu explained. And so the new South Africa chose a more complex and creative "third way"[3]—in essence a national "difficult conversation."

The strategy developed for reconciliation drew heavily on values both Christian and Bantu, the dominant tribal culture of black South Africa. The new government created a process that gave legal priority to victims who had been silenced

45

and sidelined. In what became a safe place, they were able to confront their former oppressors. Those who had participated in the apartheid system were offered amnesty on the condition that they listen to the stories told by those who had suffered as a result of the oppressors' actions, and then tell the truth about what had occurred. Participation was entirely voluntary—many of the perpetrators chose not to participate in the program but to take their chances in the courts instead. Sometimes those who faced their former victims told conflicting stories that could not be corroborated, or blatantly lied about what they had done. Still, for two years the Truth and Reconciliation Commission, convened by Archbishop Tutu, made it possible for some dramatic and transformative conversations to occur. Tutu wrote that the process itself was exhausting in every way: physically, emotionally, and spiritually. At times the graphic descriptions of heartless torture left few dry eyes in the room, and the archbishop would pause for prayer or to lead the singing of a hymn. But through the process, hidden truths came to light. Heavy burdens of sinful action were confessed, and sometimes forgiveness was offered. Healing began not just for the individuals who participated but for the whole nation. Denial was no longer an option, and the new country began to move beyond the bitterness. The reconciliation that started through these public conversations made it possible for the new country to move forward with some integrity, blacks and whites together tackling the challenges of the future they shared.

The South African context seems far from life in North American congregations. Our issues are not nearly so dramatic. Still, there is much to learn from this courageous experiment in South Africa.

1. Difficult conversations do not

often happen on their own. Sometimes they are possible only within a process or structure that provides some sense of security for all participants.

2. Embarking on such a process needs to take place in the context of covenant—one that reflects commitments to God and the community as well as to the individuals within it. Participants need to know that there is a higher purpose to these conversations and that they are in this struggle together.

3. Hard work is to be expected. Denial and avoidance are perpetuated for a very good reason: difficult conversations are arduous and discomforting.

4. There is much at stake, including the unity of a community and the integrity of its life together. But the risk to undertake what can be an uncomfortable or painful process is well worth the effort.

Congregational Models

In any congregation there are a myriad of sticky issues brewing. We put our energies into *not* discussing them. These topics can center on potential conflicts within the congregation itself or issues from the community or culture at large. The congregation's first task is to identify a focus for such conversations; that is, what are members not talking about but should be? Then members need to decide what model of conversation makes sense for them. One creative church organized a "controversial issues committee" for this very purpose: to identify what should be on the congregation's agenda and what type of format would work best. Members could suggest topics with which they thought the congregation should grapple. Sometimes suggestions came in anonymously on slips of paper. Part of the genius of this simple process is that it communicates by its very name that "We know controversial issues are out there." By forming a designated committee, the church offers a clear entry point for getting issues on the table.

Congregations have come up with a variety of models of structuring difficult conversations. No one model is better than all others. A process that works once for a congregation may not provide the best approach to another issue. Every context is different. But figuring out the right approach can make all the difference in the quality of the conversations.

The models share some common elements. First, it is not assumed that consensus will result. Rather, a higher value is placed on understanding and acceptance rather than agreement. Second, all the models described provide a safe environment, so that participants do not have to fear ridicule, ostracism, breach of confidentiality, or disrespect. These dimensions of covenant making were not left to chance or the assumption of good intentions on everyone's part. Wisely, these models all reflect wisdom and intentionality in setting up the process.

Congregational Forum

Often churches that do want to address an issue decide to hold a forum or series of forums on a topic. Leaders take care to find representatives from differing perspectives so that the program is "balanced." The goal is to expose members to different positions so that individually they can make up their own minds and act according to conscience. This kind of event is not a bad thing—but it is not necessarily conversational. The process is oriented more to sharing information than to fostering deliberation.

Congregational forums, however, can become an occasion for dialogue rather than passive listening. Such was the case at Church of the Covenant in Boston when the use of gender-inclusive language became a point of tension in the congregation. Some women had felt excluded by the overwhelming use of masculine pronouns for God in the worship service. Others were angered by the prospect of changing the traditional (and familiar) language of the liturgy. In the worship committee tempers flared when discussion focused on the Lord's Prayer.

Instead of ignoring the issue, referring it to the staff or church board to decide, or letting the faction with the most votes prevail, the worship committee decided to structure a series of congregational meetings. Members who felt strongly about the topic presented carefully prepared papers as grist for the congregational conversation. The pre-sentations and resulting discussions focused on deeply held commitments to tradition and personal images of God. Members shared their experiences of prayer and the meanings attached to the symbolic language of "father" and "mother." Far from being a superficial struggle over political correctness, this congregational conversation reflected profound theological complexity and integrity. Finally, one wise woman observed, "We've just spent six weeks talking about that split second between 'our' and 'who.' Remember, Jesus gave the prayer in response to a request to teach them how to pray, not what to pray." The members then initiated a process for allowing themselves to be taught by the Lord's Prayer. The resolution in this case was one of practice rather than agreement, one that acknowledged and respected the diversity of perspectives in the congregation. The traditional language was used once a month, on communion Sundays. Parishioners wrote a collection of prayers modeled on the Lord's Prayer for all other weeks.

This forum series was a success on many levels. A potential conflict was not allowed either to brew destructively or to erupt into a nasty church fight. Rather, differing perspectives and dearly held commitments were aired, explored, and resolved. More important, the resolution itself became a creative process out of which the theological understanding of all participants was deepened. In this safe space, members had learned to deal with diversity, and to draw on their experience and understanding of the faith to come to a place of compromise that had integrity for everyone. The educational impact made a ripple extending far beyond that moment in a congregation's life.

Conversation in Small Groups

St. Vincent's Roman Catholic Church in Philadelphia exudes good intentions on issues of justice. In the language of its vibrant liturgy, the images used in well-crafted sermons, and a survey of mission activities, the parish's commitment to racial justice is clear. But the demographic contrast between the church and its neighborhood became uncomfortable for parishioners. Located in a predominantly African American section of the city, this dynamic church had in recent years attracted a congregation that was overwhelmingly white. The clergy and lay leaders of St. Vincent's wanted to enhance the growing diversity of the congregation. Taking up the question of whether the church should become a "racial healing zone," leaders realized that this was not even a decision for the faith community to make. The Rev. Aidan Rooney remembers, "When we realized that it was not a question of if but how we could become a racial healing zone, then the thing began to march." St. Vincent's decided to structure what would surely be difficult conversations for the congregation on the issue of race. Moving from issues addressed abstractly in sermons to sustained personal conversation would a big step indeed.

Conveners were chosen from the congregation and trained to lead small groups on racial healing. Failing to find resources that met its needs, St. Vincent's developed its own workbook, complete with thought-provoking articles and weekly questions for reflection. Throughout the fall, 19 groups of six to eight participants met for eight weeks. The multiracial groups focused on assumptions they had about other racial groups, the ways that bias could subtly infiltrate both

church and culture, and the ways racism had become institutionalized. There were awkward moments, to be sure. Participants struggled to put into words the ideas that had remained unexpressed. They had to take risks in trying out new ways of seeing themselves and their social reality in light of the Gospel ideal of the "beloved community."

As with the small groups that were part of the seminary course mentioned in chapter 1, the St. Vincent's program had some ground rules. Confidentiality had to be assured and continually reaffirmed. Only in such a context can real, honest dialogue occur. In summer 2000, at Mideast peace negotiations at Camp David between Ehud Barak and Yasir Arafat, the media blitz preceding the meeting suddenly ceased as those ten days of conversation took place in the context of a news blackout. A policy of confidentiality becomes an essential part of the covenantal relationship clarified at the start of difficult conversations. After all, part of what makes difficult conversation so uncomfortable is that there has not been enough trust to allow people to talk before. Trust has to be constructed.

Agreeing that only one person will speak at a time and listening respectfully sound like commonsense guidelines for any social interaction. Still, it is important to identify such important values as ground rules, especially in conversation about topics on which passions can run high. Groups need to define for themselves the range of expression considered civil and appropriate. This is not to say that conversation partners will not experience anger and should not express it. Anger needs to be expressed in a context in which it can be heard and does not become a weapon for hurting others.

Setting ground rules is easier at the beginning of a difficult conversation than in the thick of discussion. Groups should decide at the outset when and where to meet and for how long. For some, it is important to rotate leadership duties. Some develop rituals for opening and closing their sessions—songs, prayers, or readings, for example. One student group wrote its own covenant of trust and read it aloud together at the beginning of each session. From the easiest to decide (meeting time) to the hardest to enforce (listening respectfully), ground rules are essential in creating safe boundaries for difficult conversation.

There are other ways to encourage dialogue so that we can move through our avoidance into the reflective conversation. Groups might decide to base their conversations on a workbook or other agreed-upon readings. Books, magazine articles, and newspaper clippings provide a common focus beyond the human experience represented in the group.

Working on case studies recounting the experience of others enables us to practice empathy and analysis which we can later call on when sharing our own stories.

Perhaps group members will feel that they need to be more educated about an issue and decide to invite a speaker with expertise to provide background information. Films and videos can provoke lively discussion and help us to see issues from a different angle. Keeping journals helps participants to continue working through their thoughts between group meetings.

Group leaders can either be permanently designated or rotated within the group. The convener must keep many elements in mind: ground rules, format, methods of both moving conversation toward greater levels of understanding, and tactics to maintain civility. Alice and Bob Evans, founders of Plowshares Institute (an organization that teaches

conflict-resolution skills), use case studies as the entrée into discussions of complex issues. One of their more effective strategies is to encourage participants to engage in a discipline of repeating the last speaker's arguments before making their own response. For example, rather than just launching into my defense of public schools, I would need to preface my remarks by reiterating the argument of the previous speaker. "So you believe parochial school is the wiser choice because you feel that small class size is better for children." This exercise has the effect of forcing us to listen to what others are saying rather than using their airtime to formulate our next monologue. It also helps the listener to focus a response to a particular concern. But as the Evanses point out in their training, something happens when you have to articulate the position of another, putting that speaker's words in your mouth.

53

However much we may disagree, this small act opens the possibility that we can empathize with another perspective. While we might never come to agreement, our empathy and understanding can transform a whole community as well as the individuals in it.

After the initial conversation or series of conversations has been completed, many groups decide to become an ongoing entity. If this reaction reflects a desire to stay on the mountaintop—that is, wanting to hang onto the experience itself and not believing that it could be replicated in other settings—leaders should encourage that conversation to end so that others can take place. But sometimes small groups wish to continue in order to take the conversation further or to move into transformative action.

Ongoing Conversations

Perhaps the best known among structured, ongoing small groups, and representing some of the most difficult conversations, are the various 12-step recovery programs: Alcoholics Anonymous, Narcotics Anonymous, Gamblers Anonymous, Al-Anon, and so forth. Much has been written about these movements, and religious institutions would do well to learn from them what makes their ministries so effective. That larger discussion is beyond the scope of this book. But what is worth looking at here is how 12-step groups sustain such difficult conversation and why members keep showing up, knowing that the process could be painful, confrontational, and brutally honest.

A few of the elements of conversation mentioned earlier are essential parts of 12-step programs. Meetings begin with ritual—in this case, first-name introductions followed by an admission of the shared struggle of addiction. "I'm Judy, and I'm an alcoholic." "I'm Tom, and I'm a drug addict." The purpose of the circle of introductions is to establish a sense of community. Social divisions of class, race, gender, age, or sexual orientation melt as a common experience and common humanity bond the strangers together.

Confidentiality is critical to the success of 12-step programs, as it is with all difficult conversations. It is only in the context of trusting that identities will not be revealed nor struggles shared outside the meeting that participants are free to be honest with themselves and each other. Trusting that everyone is working toward the same goal of recovery enables group members to confront one another and then follow up with contacts between meetings. Everyone knows how it feels to "hit the bottom," as well as how

tough it is to stop addictive behaviors and put a life back together. Participants know that honesty with themselves and others is critical to recovery. The covenant they make with one another, with a "higher power," and with themselves is what finally enables transformation to occur. Lives are changed—often dramatically—and the commitment to a process of difficult conversations makes that possible.

When we come together in trust and openness to real dialogue, we will be changed to some degree in the encounter. The problem is that, unlike those coming to AA groups out of an acknowledged need for change, we avoid difficult conversations because we don't want to change. Our minds are made up. We know where we stand, and we assume we know what the other will say—so why bother? Unlike committed members of recovery groups, we view each other not in terms of commonality, but through the lens of difference. Why would I want to talk with this *other*, this *not-me*?

Ongoing small-group conversation is rich but hard to sustain for those with such a mind-set. Difficult conversation can be transformative and take us into places we have not imagined—but not if we don't want to go there. One congregation in an East Coast city held dear its commitment to tolerance and inclusivity. These values had led members to take courageous public positions on several issues, including homosexuality. Some of their actions had drawn the ire of activists within the faith community who opposed their stands on the ordination of gays and lesbians and advocacy for domestic-partners legislation. Seeking reconciliation within the wider religious community, they decided to establish a relationship with their brothers and sisters in the faith who had angrily condemned them. Perhaps ongoing dialogue could result in real reconciliation.

A prominent representative of a faith-based organization that declared homosexuality to be incompatible with the intentions of God was invited to the church. He brought another member of his group who sat quietly with his Bible in his lap, a role which he later admitted was to make sure the speaker remained on message. What the host church had hoped would become a difficult conversation ended up as an awkward monologue. The guest spoke without interruption, passionately explaining his organization's position on gay rights. The group listened patiently and asked a few polite questions at the end. The guest had hoped to win converts to his side—although realistically he knew that would probably not happen. Members of the host church felt silenced and intimidated. They could not find common ground on which to build—even their perspectives on the faith they shared were painfully different, to the point of mutual exclusion. Dialogue did not happen, and reconciliation became an even more distant dream as participants walked away more alienated than before the encounter. Ongoing dialogue was not even a possibility. Neither change nor trust was risked, and the dream of recovering community in the midst of diversity was, once again, a dream deferred. This congregation has continued the dialogue about homosexuality among its own members, but the bridging conversations with the larger community of faith are still a challenge.

While sustaining ongoing difficult conversations marked by vitality and integrity is tougher than running time-limited programs, such an outcome is not impossible. In fact, making the conversation an ongoing part of a congregation's life should be a goal.

At St. Vincent's, it was clear that what began as eight-week discussion groups would become an ongoing commitment. The expressions of that commitment changed, as did the formats of dialogue. But, as will be seen in the next chapter, the conversation continued. Participants in the discussion groups found at the end of the program that they simply could not go back to where they had been before eight weeks of difficult conversations on race. They had been changed as individuals and members of the faith community. There was no turning back. They had to continue working on the problem of racism.

Whether the format is an ongoing conversation, a time-limited small group, or a one-time forum, it must be acknowledged that difficult conversations change people. That change cannot be predicted much less controlled. We can and should enter into difficult conversations knowing what some of the outcomes might be, as well as remaining open to the unexpected consequences of the Spirit at work in the people of God.

57

Questions for Discussion

1. Follow two or three current issues in the news closely for several weeks—local as well as regional and national.

- Who are the spokespersons for opposing positions, or a range of positions?
- What values can you identify that might be informing their positions?
- Which of the proponents, pundits, or commentators speak from a faith perspective that can be identified?
- Which of these issues have been discussed in your congregation, in either informal or structured conversation?

2. If your congregation had a "controversial issues committee," what topics might be suggested to it, perhaps anonymously?

3. A number of approaches are identified as contexts for difficult conversations, including congregational forums and small groups that meet for a specified or indeterminate period of time. Think of an issue for your congregation. In what context might difficult conversations best be cultivated?

4. In a congregation described at the end of the chapter, high hopes for a difficult conversation with opposing perspectives on homosexuality fizzled and instead became an "awkward monologue."

- How might this situation have been avoided?

- What could the host committee have done by way of preparation?
- What could have happened differently in the encounter itself?
- What follow-up would you suggest to the church?

CHAPTER 5

What's the Point?

When we grapple with complex issues honestly and openly, when we can act in trust and take some risks, when we enter into con versations that we know will be difficult, we will not emerge unchanged. As we have said earlier, we recognize at some deep level that transformation is a result of difficult conversations, and that is one reason we would rather not go down that road. But let's say we have, as a congregation, taken the leap and begun such dialogue. We have committed ourselves to engage each other on some painful issues. We have plunged into exploring perspectives that are still forming. We stumble awkwardly through a new language, fearing that our differences may be irreconcilable. But now what? Why are we putting ourselves through this pain? What's the point? What is the change that will come out of the effort?

For many congregations, just talking is considered enough. We feel as if we have actually done something just by discussing it—whether the subject is hunger, racism, public education, or domestic violence. Mainline Protestants have been particularly vulnerable to the illusion that talk is action. Denominations have debated social-policy issues and made pronouncements or issued statements. They have churned out curricula to guide education, reflection, and dialogue on tough issues. The results of such educational initiatives have been admirable: participants have seen their understanding expand and even their attitudes change. But too often, we stop there. The assumption is that the saints have been equipped now to go and follow their individual consciences "in the world." Some do, but for most, talk does not translate into action. At least we've done *something*—isn't it enough?

Headlines scream that yet another violent incident has taken place, this time in a school closer by. Fearful parents have begun to demand changes in gun laws, making it more difficult for a 13-year-old to find and use a semiautomatic weapon. The National Rifle Asso-

ciation responds that we must protect constitutional rights and that weapons are not the source of violence—there are other social and spiritual forces at work. The two views seem mutually exclusive, and both sets of values resonate with most Americans. There is a philosophical and political standoff. But clearly something has to change—the situation is intolerable. Kids are killing themselves and each other. It is not enough to say to ourselves, "This is a difficult issue. We discussed it at church." Something must be done.

Beyond Talk

Stephen Carter, legal scholar and perceptive social analyst, describes the meaning of *integrity* in his book of the same name.[1] He draws on the work of theologian Dietrich Bonhoeffer, who wrestled with his own conscience as a man of faith in Germany during World War II. In his eventual decision to support an assassination attempt on Hitler— a decision that cost him his life— he became consumed with the question of integrity. For Bonhoeffer and Carter, integrity is not a virtue or singular moment in time. Rather, integrity is a three-step process for an individual.

First, one must research an issue as thoroughly as one is able. This step includes gathering facts and becoming familiar with differing perspectives and positions on an issue. Too often we begin the dialogue with ourselves or one another without knowing the facts. Before engaging the issue of, say, welfare reform, we must first know what we are dealing with. How many people are on welfare? What benefits are available? What does welfare reform mean in practice? How does the legislative policy translate into social-service delivery? How will eligibility requirements change, and what will be the impact? What needs will no longer be met by the state, and how will they be addressed? What has been the experience of other states in scaling back on public subsidies for poor families? Who represents various perspectives on welfare reform and what are they saying? What do welfare recipients say? The commitment to doing our homework first about an issue can be daunting. After all, some specialists devote entire careers to researching and understanding an issue as complex as welfare. But the discipline of entering into an issue by first becoming educated about it is critical. Although it represents a significant investment of time, consider the alternatives: either we venture into an issue without really understanding what we are talking about (and therefore lose our credibility), or we are overwhelmed by the complexity of a topic

63

of public interest and opt out altogether. Either way, the conversations, which are so foundational to democracy, suffer.

Integrity demands that we not stop there. As we begin to understand an issue more clearly and bring our faith to bear as a resource, the second movement of integrity requires that we act on what we have come to know. What action we need to take will become clearer as we become more informed and engage others within our faith community.

The third step in the process of integrity is then to articulate what we have done and why. We value the sanctity of the voting booth in the United States. Trusting that only we will know how we mark the ballot is an important component of freedom. But acting on conscience only in secret does not constitute integrity. After Bonhoeffer was imprisoned, he felt a moral responsibility to own the controversial stand he had taken—to seek a violent resolution to Hitler's reign of terror—and to interpret it in his writings. Any action that is to have a public impact is no longer an individual act. In a democratic society we rail against public-policy decisions made behind closed doors. Accountability is an essential part of an open and dynamic public process.

Just so, communities of faith should not hide their lights under bushels. We need also to be held accountable for the actions we take. When difficult conversations lead us to understand an issue, and to choose what action we must take, integrity demands that we bear witness to what we have done and why. If we feel disinclined to interpret our actions publicly, we must ask ourselves why. Are we ashamed of what we have done? Are we unsure? Are we afraid of offending others or risking the alienation of our supporters?

Then we have to question whether these concerns are legitimate. The action that comes out of difficult conversations must also be discussed. Otherwise, integrity is lacking.

Unexpected Outcomes

The process of integrity, as described by Stephen Carter, is a compelling and logical model. Through the education and discernment process, an appropriate action response becomes clear. Action is taken and interpreted. However, what is clear in theory becomes painfully complicated in reality, especially when the process of conversation, action, and reflection involves other people. To be sure, well-planned actions can grow out of difficult conversations, and such expected outcomes should be a goal of the process. But like the unpredictable dynamics of conversation itself, more changes can result that surprise even the most

conscientious and well-prepared program planners. Such is the delightful nature of the Spirit when given room to work in human community.

As St. Vincent's Church began its difficult conversations around racial healing, members envisioned that at the end of the process the congregation would be more attractive to people of color and that the congregation's demographics would begin to reflect more closely the make-up of the neighborhood. In fact, three years after the racial healing initiative was begun, significant change is visible. As Father Aidan Rooney looks out at the sea of faces gathered each week for the 11:30 A.M. mass he has seen a rainbow emerge. "It used to be only about 10 percent of those at that mass were persons of color. Now it's more like 40 to 50 percent!" A clear, anticipated, quantifiable goal is being met. But that statement only begins to tell the story of transformation at St. Vincent's. The congregation experienced changes far beyond what parishioners thought they had bargained for going into the process.

It must be noted that even for this congregation, which is considered liberal and tolerant, the conversations were certifiably difficult. After an initial stage of politeness, participants moved into a phase that parish ministries coordinator Dick Taylor labeled as "chaos and emptiness."[1]

> This comes when people determine to break through the superficiality, voice their opinions and face the real issues that racism raises. Conflict emerges. Emotions of anger and trepidation come out. Participants feel that they are going backward, away from loving community. The problems raised seem overwhelming or unsolvable. But if people can hang on through the "chaos" stage, undergo self-examination, share fears and vulnerabilities, admit prejudices, express willingness to change and speak the truth in love, chaos can give way to stage three—*real community.*[2]

The planners of the process did remain flexible, adding workshops and more support for group leaders. Professional "diversity trainers" were consulted, and one joined the leadership group. For those who could not commit to an eight-week process, a more intensive weekend conference was held, with mixed reactions. Those overseeing the program prayed a lot. The process did not go exactly as they had envisioned it would—nor had they anticipated all the outcomes.

- Individual participants came to terms with the reality of white privilege, which began to affect their own sense of vocation. Some who had settled in homogeneous suburban communities moved back into racially diverse city neighborhoods because of what they had learned in the conversations about themselves, the cost of segregation in urban neighborhoods, and the role of the church as an agent of racial reconciliation.

- The parish itself was challenged and changed. The congregation had to examine who the parish leaders were and how they were chosen. More people of color were incorporated into the central leadership of the church.

- Participants realized that their physical space did not reflect a commitment to racial reconciliation. The parish hall renovation was affected by the conversations, ensuring that the space would become better suited to the needs of neighborhood programs. Sacred art around the church was evaluated in light of what it communicated; consequently more Afrocentric art was added.

- Liturgy had always been a strong suit at St. Vincent's, magnetically attracting white Catholics from more than 70 ZIP code areas. But as a result of the conversations on racial healing, more Afrocentric music and liturgical expressions were incorporated to reflect the commitments and vision of the congregation.

- The transforming consciousness of the congregation led members outside their walls and into the public square in new ways. A group of volunteers journeyed to Mississippi to help rebuild a church that had been torched by racial hatred. (The group continues to go to other sites each summer.) The church was also

67

led into advocacy on behalf of an African-American man wrongly accused of a crime and jailed. They took a next step to advocate more broadly for fairness in the judicial system.

- Father Rooney reported that the veterans of these difficult conversations on race found their political agenda expanding to other issues, including justice for women. Because conversational muscles had been exercised and they had learned to "withstand discomfort," they could more actively engage one of the most difficult issues for Catholics—women's ordination.

The overall effect of the difficult conversations has not been a linear progression in which A led to B and one could predict that C would follow. Rather, like concentric circles on a pond's surface rippling from a central point of impact, effects of the conversations radiated outward. Their impact has at once affected individuals, society, and the church itself. Consistent with the admonitions of Dietrich Bonhoeffer and Stephen Carter, the integrity of the conversations is best known through their outcomes. The members of St. Vincent's have moved beyond talk and education to publicly interpreted action. And the ripples continue.

Smart Outcomes

Even though it is realistic and desirable to allow conversations to lead to actions that could not have been anticipated at the outset, this is not to say that we relinquish all control. As difficult conversations move from the struggling phase St. Vincent's recognized as "chaos" to asking, "Now what?" congregations can ease the transition from talk to action by being smart about what outcomes make the most sense.

It has first to be determined whether, in fact, a group response is possible. A group has emerged from conversations on homosexuality profoundly moved by personal stories of participants, and with greater understanding of those whose positions they had once dismissed out of hand. A deeper sense of community is a precious outcome of all the hard work. Group members all want to move "beyond talk," with some now feeling empowered to advocate for the inclusion of gay and lesbian people in all aspects of the church's life and leadership. Other group members simply can't go there, but now appreciate and respect the commitments of those who would. Collective action on the part of this discussion group is not possible, but group members have not failed. Crossing ideological boundaries so that they are now able to pray together is grace in itself. Their

integrity will be measured by how their new understanding is expressed in action, even if they do not act as a collective whole. It is important that congregations enter into difficult conversations knowing that consensus will not necessarily be the outcome.

But consider the radical possibility that collective action might be possible, even when not everyone in the group is in complete agreement. Citizens who emerge from sequestered juries often describe their experience as a powerful process of coming to agreed-upon action from a variety of perspectives. More often than not, juries constitute what becomes a structured difficult conversation, and collective action is the expected outcome. It is surprising that so few juries are "hung" and unable to come to agreement. In interpreting their decision, many jurors speak of the depth of struggle and continuing differences in perspective throughout the process. The subsequent decision comes as relief and can feel empowering to former strangers who were essentially forced to find enough agreement to take action. While isolating a conversation group from the congregation is not the model being offered here, it is important to keep in mind that individuals can come to *enough* consensus to take action, even while respecting a diversity of perspectives.

When formulating a response to the "now what?" question, a smart outcome is an action that *makes sense* for the congregation. That is to say, the congregation's own culture, resources, and style have to be considered. At St. Vincent's a number of the decisions focused on the liturgy—a strategy that makes sense in a congregation where worship life is of central value. The action also has to also make sense in terms of the issue itself and context in which the action will be taken. Strategies such as marching on Washington,

writing letters to the editor, and developing an organization or agency are all valid in and of themselves, but are effective only when they make sense in terms of who the congregants are, the nature of the issue, and the context in which the people will act.

One small urban congregation, made up predominantly of older members, struggled to better understand and express their sense of mission. In small groups, members had confronted the reality of hunger, not only in other countries but also in their own neighborhood. Out of a series of difficult conversations on the maldistribution of resources, congregants were moved to respond in a way that made absolute sense for this congregation: they collected grocery-store coupons and attempted to distribute them to the neighborhood. Unfortunately, the strategy made no sense in light of the issue and the context: young mothers on welfare were not inclined to approach the unfamiliar church that had had such a low profile in the community for so long. Even if they had, they could not use the coupons with their food stamps in local stores at that time. Besides, it taxed the imagination to see how getting a dollar off the price of dog food or coffee was addressing global hunger.

The coupon program was not a smart outcome in many ways. Had the members engaged the issue in more detail, they would have realized that what might make sense for them didn't necessarily make sense for the recipients. What had attracted them to this action, however, was that it was doable.

Sociologists who study social movements have for the past 30 years tried to identify the factors that lead to collective social action. A number of conditions for social mobilization have been identified: griev-ance ("This is wrong"), moral imperative ("We've got to do something"), resources available (money and people), and a shift in political opportunities ("The mayor has been voted out of office"), among them. Stanford researcher Doug McAdam studied the civil rights movement extensively and found that in fact all these factors are present in that definitive social movement. But alone or even together, they are not enough. In McAdam's analysis,[3] the critical variable that spurs people beyond talk to action is a *sense of viability*. When people begin to see that they could take action (feasibility) and that their action would be effective in bringing about the change they seek, collective social action begins to happen.

As difficult conversations move toward active response, it is important that congregations cultivate a sense of viability. A strategy might make sense and be well within the

71

realm of possibility for the church. But is it feasible? Will it be both effective and a faithful response to a troubling situation? Call the sense of viability a type of hope, if you will—an informed hope. Sometimes congregations are encouraged by the actions of others and model their own action accordingly. Sometimes viability is enhanced by joining with other congregations.

Recent years have seen an explosive growth of faith-based community organizing networks. Congregations that want to take faithful and effective action on political issues find that by joining with others, they expand their power base. One of the most difficult of conversations concerns the relationship between a city and its suburbs. At first blush the topic might seem to be of interest only to "policy wonks." But try engaging church members on both sides of a city's boundaries in a discussion about sharing regional resources for public education and transportation. Passions quickly come to the surface, and a conversation can stop dead in its tracks. This dynamic is in no way different from what happens in discussions on the issue of regionalism among municipal governments and community groups. Social-class tensions come to the surface, and an undercurrent of race haunts almost every discussion—albeit under the surface.

Yet a closer study of the issue indicates that cities and suburbs need each other for their very survival. Getting to this point is easy; deciding what to do about it is difficult. The question seems overwhelming in its complexity. Some of the brightest policy architects are working on the issue, and experiments in regionalism are popping up around the country. But urbanologist David Rusk has found that one of the most effective strategies in getting city and suburban folk to talk to each other and recognize their common destinies is through regional networks of congregations. In his book *Inside Game, Outside Game*,[4] Rusk describes how one regional faith-based network in Indiana was able not only to engage this difficult conversation as congregations, but also to create a context for the major players from throughout the region to sit down at the table. These congregations were smart because they recognized the viability of regional change and then maximized the possibility by working together. As a result, city and suburbs were able to work together in resolving a land-use conflict to everyone's advantage.

Developing a Plan of Action

We have discussed a number of considerations for congregations that want to move smartly beyond talk and beyond the good intentions that can result in noble but ineffectual action. We need to ask: Does this action make sense in light of who we are, what the issue is, and the context in which we speak? Is it doable? Is it an effective strategy? Should we work alone or in a coalition? Other questions must be answered as well: Who should lead this effort? How long and to what extent will we keep going?

One of the most critical considerations in embarking on a course of action is in the choice between service and activism. To introduce the topic of domestic violence into a class or church group is to see the anxiety level rise visibly. Of course "good church people" are outraged by the idea of wives being beaten by their husbands, or children being abused by parents. But few families have not been touched by violence at home in some way. Enormous emotional energy goes into keeping

73

secret such family dynamics, and so introducing the topic becomes threatening and painful. Conversation must be entered into cautiously, because there will be a high degree of vulnerability on the part of some participants.

Moving through the difficult conversation to a point of wanting to respond poses another choice: Should we choose to minister to those who are victims, or to work as advocates to change the laws and allocation of resources? The faith community has been in the forefront of both types of efforts—establishing shelters for battered women and advocating for easier access to restraining orders for women at risk, for example. One strategy is palliative, the other preventive in light of human suffering. To follow only one tack is always to feel inadequate because we are either ignoring the victim or applying only Band-Aid solutions. Ideally, communities of

faith can balance their actions between the two approaches, but that is not always possible with limited resources. Smart congregations recognize the possibility of ongoing tension between the desires to serve and to advocate.

An infinite range of possible outcomes arises from difficult conversations. Some are expected and planned for; others catch us by surprise. It is important to allow the Spirit to change us in ways we didn't expect—and to celebrate that. It is also important to move from conversation to action with our eyes open, so that the energy generated in our encounter with one another can be focused in creative action rather than dissipating. Ideally, the conversation and the action should keep going.

Questions for Discussion

1. Recall a moment of real integrity in a congregation or community group—that is, a time when a difficult issue was investigated and action was taken and publicly interpreted.

- What were some of the elements that made it work?—leadership, hope, or resources, for example.
- What are some of the unexpected results that have occurred since?

2. The outcomes described in the St. Vincent's case study are varied and positive. Yet fears of negative outcomes fuel our avoidance of difficult conversations. Imagine some negative outcomes that might have occurred at St. Vincent's as a result of its structured conversation on racism.

3. Identify a topic for difficult conversation in your congregation.

- What type of format might make sense both in light of who you are and the nature of the issue to be discussed?
- Imagine what some of the outcomes might be, including hoped-for, positive, and negative outcomes.

CHAPTER 6

Keeping the Conversation Going

It may seem ironic to spend so much time considering difficult conversations at a time when talk shows dominate much of radio and TV programming. We have considered the strategies we employ in our churches to avoid such conversations and methods to recover the lost art of talking together about the tough issues that confront our families, communities, congregations, and nation. Yet we can turn on the TV anytime, night or day, and witness people wading into the most difficult of topics:

- Family members confronted with the sexual behaviors of one another
- Audiences vigorously reacting to those who defend corporate policies
- Public officials squirming in their interaction with a probing journalist

From the raucous antics of Jerry Springer, to the witty repartee of "Politically Incorrect," to the more dignified "Nightline," it would seem that the media are saturated with difficult conversations. A visitor to North America at the beginning of the 21st century might well assume that it is characteristic of this culture to place a high value on intense engagement around knotty

77

issues and that most citizens are adept at engaging these issues.

Wrong! The predominance of TV and radio talk shows can quite possibly be explained not by who we are but by who we aren't. That is to say, it is because we are *inept* at difficult conversation that we have found ways to package it in a show-biz format. We consume these shows voyeuristically, as a form of entertainment. In other words, difficult conversation is so rare in everyday life that we tune in out of curiosity to view it as a kind of spectacle. When we consider even the more subdued talk shows, it is clear that we as a culture consider truly difficult conversation to be a remarkable and newsworthy art.

It is no wonder that we would want to avoid difficult conversations, which, on television at least, can look more like professional wrestling. What I am proposing is the possibility in congregations of conversation that is honest and risk-taking, yet civil and respectful. The model is not combative or competitive; it is one that leads participants to mutual transformation and growth. Certainly when congregations can enable such conversation to take place around hard issues, they do more than strengthen the bonds of the visible church. They also counter an unhealthy trend toward isolation in the wider culture and contribute social capital essential to a robust democracy.

The challenge before us is to move beyond our own packaging of difficult conversation into digestible units, and to integrate it into our life together. How can we move difficult conversation beyond a structured eight-week series to become part of the congregation's culture? How can it shift from being an anomaly in our congregational life to becoming the norm? How do we move from event to habit?

Cultivating Conversation

Certainly the skills learned in structured conversations within the congregation's life are transferable to other contexts within the church, the community, and our personal lives. Just as those in the St. Vincent's dialogues on race learned how to "withstand discomfort" in addressing other issues, we learn in difficult conversations about ourselves and others. We learn to explore ideas and to listen respectfully. We learn to appreciate our own values and the guiding principles of others. We discover that we can move through topics we have spent lifetimes avoiding and not be destroyed in the process—or cause relationships and community to be destroyed. If we're lucky, we open ourselves to learning more about how the Spirit of God moves in and through the people of God. This process is what I have called exercising our conversational muscles.

But the exercise needs to continue, or the muscles will become weak and flabby again. We need to find ways to reinforce the value and to support the opportunity for further conversation. As with anything that resists the flow of the dominant culture, the key word is *persistence*. We cannot trust a single experience to bring permanent change, or to continue the change that has begun, without sustained effort. We cannot expect the memory of a positive experience or the resolutions it generates in the participants to suffice. If in fact we have come to value difficult conversation as an important ingredient of a truly democratic society, an invigorated congregation, and an individual life of integrity, then we have to incorporate it intentionally into our life together. But how? Here I would like to begin—and only begin—thinking creatively by suggesting three areas where difficult conversation might begin to find a permanent home in a congregation's life.

Conversation-Friendly Programs

Perhaps the first place most congregations think of lodging activity is in the area of program. Committees, educational programs, and retreats are all ways that congregations minister to members. Difficult conversation is somewhat different from other aspects of a congregation's ministry in that overinstitutionalization could kill it. It is hard to imagine a permanent committee devoted to the task of maintaining fresh and lively conversation. But remaining open to possible short-term programs, organized as new topics emerge, could provide a safe haven for a various difficult conversations to occur as needed. Time-limited events, groups, or forums could offer opportunities for dialogue on particular troubling issues. Any programmatic response should offer opportunity for education (that is, learning about an issue), as well as for working out our understanding of it in light of our faith. As seen in the previous chapter, both emphases are needed. We can't jump into conversation about a topic like abortion without knowing something about it medically, politically, emotionally, and sociologically. If we are not educated about an issue, and if we speak only from the perspective of our values, discussion quickly slips into sloganeering and eventual polarization. Nor can we treat such a value-laden subject clinically, offering "just the facts." We need also to deal with values, giving participants an opportunity, in a safe environment, to struggle with their deepest questions.

Identifying the agenda for difficult conversation should not be the responsibility of the leadership alone.

Anyone in the congregation should be able to make suggestions.

One model being used in some congregations is the creation of "clearness groups," originally a Quaker practice. Here, anyone who is struggling with an issue—personal, public, or both—is invited to request that a group come together for a limited period of time to help the person deal with the conflict, or come to clarity about it. A couple contemplating a cross-racial adoption needs to work through the social, political, and personal issues before proceeding. The parents of an adult daughter have just learned that she is lesbian. They need a safe place in which to learn more about homosexuality, to understand their own feelings, and to decide how then to respond as parents. A young professional is offered a high-paying promotion, but he wants to be clear about his own faith values in regard to work and money. A family

suspects that a vacant lot next to their house is being used to dump toxins, but they don't know what to do about it.

These are all familiar issues that can churn the stomachs of the people in the pews. Usually they remain "private problems," and we are left on our own to bring our faith to bear in understanding the issues and deciding how then to live. But one does not have to scratch the surface very deep to understand that none of the examples above are purely personal issues. They have social and political dimensions, as well as theological significance for the congregation. Clearness groups provide a confined, trusting environment in which faith and life come together. These are not therapy groups but opportunities for members to grow together in their understandings of the faith and in their integrity. One presents a dilemma; others who have volunteered to be part of this clearness group offer suggestions and questions to help move the person toward "clearness."

- "Have you thought about . . . ?"
- "Here's what I know about . . . "
- "Look at it from another perspective . . ."
- "It reminds me of what the Bible says . . ."

It might take only one meeting or extend over a number of weeks. When those who called for the clearness group believe that they understand the issue better and know what action they should take, then it is time for closure. When those who initiate the process risk trusting their sisters and brothers with their own struggle, they realize that in fact they are not alone. Trust breeds empowerment, and with the support that develops, action can be taken.

In difficult conversations in the congregation, flexibility remains critical. One thing can and should lead to another as the group determines that the whole congregation should grapple with an issue. A clearness group could lead to a congregational forum on adoption, a class on homosexuality, a series of sermons on work and wealth, or a petition against toxic dumping. These actions could lead to still other actions and deeper conversation. But first, we must remain open to the possibilities that we can be changed and can become agents of continuing change.

Preaching as Dialogue

Homileticians have long stressed that preaching is a form of dialogue. "Yeah, right!" the skeptic says with a shrug. Monologue, persuasive speech, and performance art come to mind as descriptors, but dialogue seems a lofty ideal or a weak apologetic. Yet preaching at its best prompts a response in the gathered congregation—either vocalized (as in many African-American churches) or unspoken. A lively dialogue can result from provocative preaching, a continuation of what was begun in the sermon.

The sermon or homily continues to occupy a central place in the weekly worship of believers across the ecumenical spectrum. It is a moment when the Word is interpreted in the context of life. A sermon represents the point in the worship experience at which human struggles and priorities can be brought into the light of the Gospel and the collective wisdom of the gathered believers. The ambiguities of human existence can then be explored with the undergirding word of God's mercy and love.

The sermon plays a role in cultivating difficult conversations in the congregation in both its form and content. There are certainly ways in which preaching itself can be restructured to resemble conversation more closely. Most members of the clergy have experimented with multiple-preacher sermons at some point in their careers—a two-person, point/counterpoint format. Such sermons can model difficult conversation, although they are labor-intensive in their preparation and are most effective when used only occasionally. The same can be said for more theatrical approaches—dramatic scenes that involve the congregation. Recently I witnessed a sermon in which the pastor impersonated a skeptic in the pew and began by stumbling into the service and clumsily finding a seat. In what was essentially improvisational theater, he spoke to those next to him and offered a running commentary on going (or not going) to church. The pastor had taken a risk, but it worked. By voicing the thoughts of many who sat facing him each week, he communicated that he understood their ambivalent feelings, and would welcome those feelings—even in church. When done well, the occasional use of drama or conversation at the sermon time can invite difficult conversation. When someone stands up during a sermon and says, "Wait a minute, preacher! What about—?" the congregation is caught off guard, and the collective tension rises. Like unscripted difficult conversation, such occasions raise fears of embarrassment and loss of control. But by the end, the congregation has had a mini-experience of surviving the risk. The message is communicated, "You can have dialogue and live."

Most preaching is more traditional and less theatrical in format. In recent years preachers in even the most staid traditions and congregations have ventured from behind the pulpit to speak more informally without notes. Most attest to the success of this experiment, and say that the format invites further conversation. Still, many clergy do not feel comfortable away from the security of a manuscript or outline. How could this more traditional approach engender difficult conversation?

Perhaps the most direct route to stimulating conversation is by preaching on those topics with which members are silently struggling. In the priestly role of going before, or representing the concerns of the people, the preacher is called to venture into what we consider scary terrain—naming those issues that smolder within us as confusing and unresolved. Looking out over the worshipers, the preacher can assume that 10 percent are gay and that perhaps a quarter have a close friend or family member who is. Most families have been "surprised" by a pregnancy; up to one-third have a family member who has had an abortion. It is difficult to know precisely what proportion of the population has been the victim or perpetrator of domestic violence (including sexual). But such violence is far more pervasive than we, as a society, ever knew or admitted. While race is a topic often in the news, people seldom talk frankly and personally about it. Even more of a rarity is honest conversation between people of different races. In her book *My First White Friend*, journalist Patricia Raybon writes movingly about a lifetime of living and working with white people but never really talking about the effect that skin color had on their lives and relationships.[1]

By bringing into the light those issues we spend energy sheltering as secrets, the preacher liberates conversation. Tension might be heightened as listeners are led into what is perceived as a dialogical minefield. But as the preacher "boldly goes where no one has gone

before" (at least in this congregation), she or he does so proclaiming the grace of God, which extends "far as the curse is found." There is no issue so controversial or painful that we cannot, in the context of the love of God, talk about it. When difficult issues are explored in a sermon, difficult conversations are possible. During the coffee hour, at home over lunch, while driving to work, the conversation continues.

There are other ways, within the sermon, that difficult conversation can be encouraged apart from engaging issues head-on. Preachers can focus on conversations within the biblical texts and look more closely at what was going on. In fact both Hebrew and Greek Scriptures provide a rich resource of recorded conversations in which the most difficult encounters were also those in which God was most clearly revealed. By preaching on these texts, the speaker communicates that

85

difficult conversation is an important component in the life of the faith community. Further, such texts affirm that conflict within these conversations is not only to be expected but that the very point of tension which we so fear becomes the opportunity for transforming grace. Think again of Jesus and his conversations with the Canaanite woman, Zacchaeus, or the rich young ruler. Of course not every difficult conversation is, in itself, transforming. But it is an important component in the ongoing revelation of who we are, who God is, and what God has to do with the complexity of life as we know it.

The preaching event is critical in the process of stimulating difficult conversations in the congregation. Here, such conversation is liberated, modeled, and affirmed. One can preach about conversation incorporating contemporary and biblical illustrations or start a dialogue by preaching on an issue that is too

often avoided. One can experiment with more dialogical forms of preaching. Any or all of these approaches can draw members to deeper levels of engagement.

Leadership and Conversation

Outside the pulpit, however, it is also critical that ministers "walk the talk." Leaders in faith communities need to exemplify a commitment to difficult conversation on a daily basis.

This commitment might mean re-evaluating the power structure within the congregation and making some changes. Shared leadership creates opportunity for more intense dialogue than does centralized power, because leaders have to negotiate perspectives and approaches. The ongoing dialogue among leaders results in continual scrutiny and evaluation of ministry—and this is a good thing! Of course, leadership teams have been known to devolve into petty power struggles. But as leaders work through issues, the quality of ministry benefits in a secondary way—by demonstrating a commitment to difficult conversation.

In relating to the congregation and community, clergy should exemplify a confidence in asking the *impertinent* questions, as well as the pertinent ones—and then following through with the conversation they hope will result. Whether writing letters to the editor, speaking at a community forum, or meeting with church members, the minister should raise those issues which, like the naked emperor, are in clear sight but considered unmentionable. Dare to ask "why"—"Why are these people unable to find work?" "Why does talking about race make us so nervous?" "Why are gay and lesbian folk feeling so threatened here?" "Why" questions lead us into the complexity of an issue and invite response, whether through telling personal stories or trying out a social analysis.

We religious leaders often feel as though we have to be consistently clear and certain in our declarations—"This is what is going on. This is what our faith says about it. That settles it!" We are better trained in prescriptive speech than in descriptive analysis. But not only is such consistent proclamation unrealistic; it is a real conversation-killer. Who wants to talk back when God has apparently spoken?

I often stress with my students of congregational studies that there is a kind of spiritual discipline in good ethnographic research. (Ethnography is the study of social behavior, largely through interviewing and participant observation.) When conducting research in a congregation, we need to recognize our well-ingrained ability to make judgments and offer proclamations. Instead we have to learn to suspend that type of normative thinking and transform it into curiosity. Instead of reacting to another's perspective judgmentally (i.e., "I can't believe she holds such heretical views!"), learn to respond with curiosity ("I wonder why she believes that? How did that perspective come about? What purpose is it serving?"). This change in the ways we respond to others is a skill, a discipline; and is important not only in research but in conversation as well.

Clergy are especially trained in, and oriented to, normative thinking, which plays a significant role in preaching and theology. But when we engage in difficult conversation, rigid normative frames don't get us far. We need to understand better the experience and perspective of the other, and curiosity will lead us there. It is not too strong to say that indeed, turning judgment into curiosity is a spiritual discipline.

What Can Go Wrong Here?

In cultivating difficult conversations in the program, worship, and life of a congregation, the sailing is not always smooth. Unexpected gusts and powerful currents seem to throw us off course or threaten to sink us altogether. But as any sailor knows, the way is seldom direct—we need to learn to tack. When encountering obstacles, congregations should try another angle. Zigzagging may not seem to be an efficient route to a goal, but it is a creative tactic. And with persistence, you will get there.

When entering into difficult conversations, anticipate what some of the obstacles might be and name your fears about the process. That way, you are better able to respond to them. What could go wrong here?

One legitimate fear is that we will be changed in the process and that we risk compromising our beliefs. In some communities of faith, it is expected that members will adhere to the "whole ball of wax." For traditional Catholics, for example, this means unquestioning acceptance of the church's teachings on papal infallibility, abortion, birth control, women's ordination, homosexuality, marriage, and divorce, as well as other articles of faith. Those who adhere selectively are considered "à la carte Catholics." Of course, Roman Catholics are not the only faith community in which some members view themselves as more orthodox than others and would offer a definitive checklist of doctrines. Baptists, Muslims, Lutherans, Presbyterians, Episcopalians, Jews, Methodists, Mormons, and others have such core groups that defend and define their understanding of the faith. Such traditionalists of any communion are not open to the possibility of difficult conversation apart from the goal of converting the other to the one true

way. An evangelistic zeal may motivate participation in a conversation, but involvement often fizzles out as soon as a standoff emerges. The hard work of active listening, deeper understanding, trust building, and risk taking is derailed as soon as the going gets tough. The unwillingness to change becomes a firewall blocking off truly engaging difficult conversation. "I am certainly not going to become an à la carte whatever!"

Even Jesus, the most patient and fearless of difficult conversation partners, taught his disciples that at times they would encounter such resistance and a legitimate response was to "shake the dust from your sandals" and move on. Whether it is the first or the 21st century, there is not much one can do at that moment.

We should remember that these cherished beliefs have historically resulted from difficult, often protracted, conversations from the personal to the denominational level.

Beliefs came out of and spoke to historical contexts. They came to hold an important and even sacred place for a people. The problem is, they came to be set in stone. Central affirmations of a faith community continue to be meaningful as they are tested against current social realities and are shown to be relevant. A religious tradition's position on such issues as abortion, homosexuality, leadership standards, and war must be continually engaged, understood, and re-evaluated in every era. Mutations will occur as the teachings evolve over time. Such changes do not necessarily mean that the faith has been hopelessly compromised or watered down, but rather that it has become socially relevant to the present age. The strongest defenders of the agenda should further keep in mind that converts are not won through coercion. It is only when we are given the opportunity to wrestle with an issue, like Jacob with the angel, that understanding and acceptance can come. But we will emerge with a new name, changed to some degree by the encounter. Communities of faith must recognize that when we deny people the opportunity for dialogue, they can become alienated and will leave.

Fear of compromise and change fuels resistance, as does the fear of dividing the congregation. In chapter 2 we visited Augustana Lutheran Church in Omaha. Conversation was silenced by the fear of splitting the congregation. Had that congregation known that its self-imposed silence would result in painful division anyway, would members have been more open to risking difficult conversation about race? Perhaps. But we can learn from their experience. Restricting the possibility of difficult conversation out of loyalty and a commitment to preserving unity might spell the beginning of the end. A church that is unwilling to discuss controversial issues is one in which unity is only skin-deep. Eventually newcomers (or old-timers, for that matter) who want to discuss tough topics will become discouraged and drift away. When issues are publicly raised, the resistance to conversation often creates more tension than the conversation itself would. Such was the case in Omaha.

Many fears feed our avoidance of difficult conversation. We fear being compromised or changed. We fear division in the house. We fear that we could be embarrassed—or worse, wounded. What if we give the zealots a forum and they come in to "cleanse the temple"? Innocent people could get hurt by their righteous rage. We could get hurt.

What are our worst fears about entering into difficult conversations? Where do we think we might encounter resistance—articulated or unspoken? It is important to name the fears and obstacles that we might encounter. This step has the effect of helping to rob fears of their power as well as enabling us to plan for difficult conversations with our eyes open.

Go for It!

Difficult conversations might begin as a sermon topic, a forum, or a time-limited series of meetings. The contexts in which they can occur are as diverse as the possible focuses. Ultimately, having such conversations should become a way of life in community—both in local faith communities and within a democratic society. It becomes a collective habit, a learned behavior. If we can condition ourselves to avoid honest dialogue about complex issues, then we can certainly learn to engage issues in ways that have integrity. That is what keeps community vital and growing.

As Christians, we dare enter what appears to be a minefield only when we affirm that we are held in the love of God. There is no human issue or struggle that cannot be brought before God, who cannot be shocked or confused or stumped by our questioning.

> For I am sure that neither
>   death, nor life
> Nor angels, nor principalities,
> Nor things present, nor things
>   to come
> Nor powers, nor height, nor
>   depth,
> Nor anything else in all cre-
>   ation
> Will be able to separate us from
>   the love of God in Christ
>   Jesus our Lord.
>   (Rom. 8: 38-39)

Indeed, humans are not intended to be robots but to bring to the table all the curiosity with which we have been created. In acknowledging God's undying acceptance of us, we are given permission to meet one another in acceptance and respect, knowing that even in disagreement there is a stronger bond not of our own making. Therefore, we are freed to "go for it."

Questions for Discussion

1. One of the strategies for "keeping the conversation going" focuses on preaching. Remember a sermon that sparked a conversation with a friend, with members of the congregation, or with the preacher. What was it about the sermon that invited you into further conversation, whether it had to do with preaching style or the content of the sermon?

2. What are the ongoing conversations in your congregation about—difficult or otherwise? What keeps them going? What are some conversation-stoppers you have noticed?

3. Put together your own "Top Ten" list of "reasons why difficult conversations don't happen in our congregations." (The reasons may be easier to identify if you are thinking about hypothetical subject matter such as race, sexuality, or poverty.)

4. Looking over your list of obstacles, consider what it would take to remove them. If you can name both the obstacles and imagine how they might be addressed, you are already well on your way to changing the habits of your church, from avoiding difficult conversations to engaging in them.

Chapter 1

1. Robert Putnam, *Bowling Alone: The Collapse and Revival of American Community* (New York: Simon & Schuster, 2000).

2. Ibid., 27.

3. Ibid., 43.

4. Ibid., 408-410.

5. Nancy Ammerman, *Congregations and Community* (New Brunswick, N.J.: Rutgers University Press, 1997).

Chapter 2

1. *A Time for Burning* produced by Lutheran Film Associates, 1966. Distributed by Gateway Films/Vision Video, P. O. Box 540, Worcester, PA 19490; (800) 523-0226; www.lutheranfilm.org The video version is available for purchase at $15.00.

2. For a discussion of bonding and bridging forms of social capital, refer to Putnam, *Bowling Alone*, chapter 1.

3. Ammerman, *Congregations and Community,* 335.

Chapter 3

1. Putnam, *Bowling Alone,* 134-147.
2. Ibid., 140-141.
3. Ibid., 142-145.
4. Ibid., 70-72.
5. Ibid., 126.
6. Ibid., 120-122.

Chapter 4

1. Desmond Tutu, *No Future Without Forgiveness* (New York: Doubleday, 1999), 29.
2. Ibid., 23.
3. Ibid., chapter 2.

Chapter 5

1. Dick Taylor, with LaVonne France, "Seven Lessons from Racial Healing at the Parish Level," *Initiative Report,* Sept. 2000.
2. Ibid., 4.
3. Doug McAdam, *Political Process and the Development of Black Insurgency, 1930-1970* (Chicago: University of Chicago Press, 1982).
4. David Rusk, *Inside Game, Outside Game: Winning Strategies for Saving Urban America* (Washington: Brookings Institution Press, 1999).

Chapter 6

1. Patricia Raybon, *My First White Friend* (New York: Viking, 1996).

$\mathcal{W}$elcome to the work of Alban Institute...
the leading publisher and congregational
resource organization for clergy and laity today.

Your purchase of this book means you have an interest in the kinds of information, research, consulting, networking opportunities and educational seminars that Alban Institute produces and provides. We are a non-denominational, non-profit 25-year-old membership organization dedicated to providing practical and useful support to religious congregations and those who participate in and lead them.

Alban is acknowledged as a pioneer in learning and teaching on *Conflict Management *Faith and Money *Congregational Growth and Change *Leadership Development *Mission and Planning *Clergy Recruitment and Training *Clergy Support, Self-Care and Transition *Spirituality and Faith Development *Congregational Security.

Our membership is comprised of over 8,000 clergy, lay leaders, congregations and institutions who benefit from:

- ❖ 15% discount on hundreds of Alban books
- ❖ $50 per-course tuition discount on education seminars
- ❖ Subscription to *Congregations*, the Alban journal (a $30 value)
- ❖ Access to Alban research and (soon) the "Members-Only" archival section of our web site www.alban.org

For more information on Alban membership or to be added to our catalog mailing list, call 1-800-486-1318, ext. 243 or write: **The Alban Institute, Attn: Membership Department, 7315 Wisconsin Avenue, Suite 1250 West, Bethesda, MD 20814-3211**